D & M Yard Services

Accounting Capstone Project

QUICKBOOKS EDITION

Darlene Schnuck

CENGAGE
Learning·

Australia • Brazil • Japan • Korea • Mexico • Singapore • Spain • United Kingdom • United States

CENGAGE Learning·

D & M Yard Services:
Accounting Capstone Project
QuickBooks Edition

Senior Manager, Student Engagement:

Linda deStefano

Janey Moeller

Manager, Student Engagement:

Julie Dierig

Marketing Manager:

Rachael Kloos

Manager, Production Editorial:

Kim Fry

Manager, Intellectual Property Project Manager:

Brian Methe

Senior Manager, Production and Manufacturing:

Donna M. Brown

Manager, Production:

Terri Daley

For product information and technology assistance, contact us at
Cengage Learning Customer & Sales Support, 1-800-354-9706

For permission to use material from this text or product,
submit all requests online at **cengage.com/permissions**
Further permissions questions can be emailed to
permissionrequest@cengage.com

Compilation © 2014 Cengage Learning

ISBN-13: 978-1-305-31193-0

ISBN-10: 1-305-31193-0

WCN: 01-100-101

Cengage Learning

5191 Natorp Boulevard
Mason, Ohio 45040
USA

Cengage Learning is a leading provider of customized learning solutions with office locations around the globe, including Singapore, the United Kingdom, Australia, Mexico, Brazil, and Japan. Locate your local office at:
international.cengage.com/region.

Cengage Learning products are represented in Canada by Nelson Education, Ltd.

For your lifelong learning solutions, visit **custom.cengage.com.**

Visit our corporate website at **cengage.com.**

Printed in the United States of America

TABLE OF CONTENTS

FOR

D & M YARD SERVICES

D&M Yard Services

This project is dedicated to my family, especially to Mike and Jamie, who have encouraged, loved, and supported me in bringing it to completion.

Many thanks to the following individuals for their time, effort, support, and expertise provided to this project: Heather Albinger, Tony Igl, my capstone course students for their continued input and the many other faculty, staff, and administrators in the Accounting department and Business lab at Waukesha County Technical College.

Dave Michaels started D & M Yard Services, a sole-proprietorship in January, 2013. The business will provide basic landscaping services and products to residential and commercial customers. You have been hired as the accountant for D & M Yard Services. You are responsible for completing all aspects of the financial accounting cycle for D & M Yard Services including year-end analysis using accounting software, and the preparation of the owner's personal income tax return using tax preparation software.

PROJECT OBJECTIVE:

The objective of this project is to serve as a capstone assessment of the following accounting program outcomes:
- ✓ Process financial transactions through the accounting cycle
- ✓ Analyze financial and business information to support decision-making and planning
- ✓ Process, report and analyze payroll
- ✓ Perform individual and business income tax preparation
- ✓ Identify internal controls

PROJECT HIGHLIGHT FEATURES:

- ✓ Students complete the entire accounting cycle WITH year-end account analysis AND preparation of business/personal income tax return (only project with all parts coordinated to one business)
- ✓ Students not only use software default forms, but also customize forms specific to business
- ✓ Students account for a WIDE variety of transactions including recurring transactions, invoicing, payroll, complaint adjustments, petty cash disbursements...
- ✓ Students account for the use of a business credit card
- ✓ Students complete payroll tax forms
- ✓ Students prepare income tax return using source documents
- ✓ Students answer monthly questions on internal controls, ethics, and financial decision-making
- ✓ Students complete a monthly task list and "To Do"

COMPANY INFORMATION:

Install Intuit QuickBooks Accountant 2013 using license and product number on program CD.

You may be prompted to register your software; just simply enter <u>any</u> answers to the questions to complete the registration.

NOTE: If you are a first-time user to QuickBooks, you will find assistance under the Help menu at QuickBooks Help as well as the Learning Center Tutorials.

Using EXPRESS START: <u>create a new sole-proprietor lawn care or landscaping company</u> for the calendar year 2013; use YOUR NAME Yard Services, e.g. Jones Yard Services, to create a file unique to you

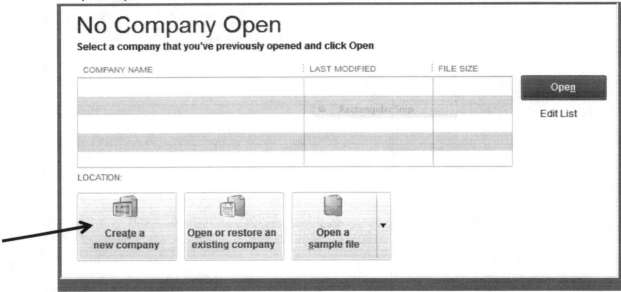

Then use the following company information:

Dave Michaels

800 Main St.

Landscape, WI 53022

262-356-2141

- Federal Employer Identification Number (EIN): 39-1212121

- Other company set-up, such as customers, vendors... will be completed when needed

Tell us about your business

Enter the essentials so we can create a company file that's just right for your business.

* Company Name	Key Yard Services	
	We'll use this on your invoices and reports, and to name your company file.	
* Industry	Lawn Care or Landscaping	Help me choose
	We'll use this to create accounts common for your industry.	
* Company Type	Sole Proprietorship ▼	Help me choose
	We'll use this to select the right tax settings for your business.	
Tax ID #	39-1212121	
	We'll use this on your tax forms.	
Do you have Employees?	Yes ▼	

* Required

📞 Need help? Give us a call

Back   Continue

Enter your business contact information

Once you enter your contact information, you're ready to create your company file.

Legal Name	D & M Yard Services
Address	800 Main St.
City	Landscape
State	WI ▼ * ZIP 53022
Country	U.S. ▼
* Phone	262-356-2141
Email	
Website	

* Required

Enter basic contact information so you can instantly print and email invoices and other forms.

This will also be used to set up your QuickBooks Payments account. We will send you an email with additional details, including how to enable your account.

We value your privacy and security. This information is stored safely on Intuit servers.

Back   Preview Your Settings   Create Company File

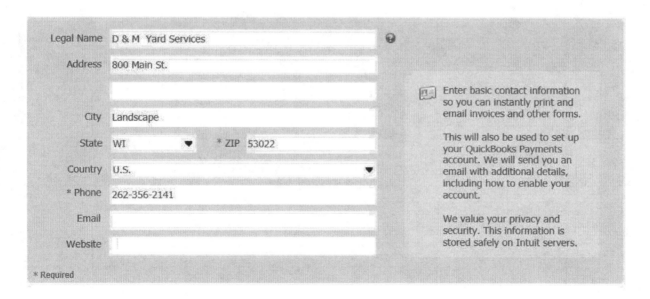

At this time, we will only add the bank account information:

D & M Yard Services Checking Acct (use YOUR NAME Yard Services and edit as necessary for the field width)

#745-1332

We will not need the QuickBooks checks.

"START WORKING"

Close "Ready to Start Working" screen to go to home page as shown below:

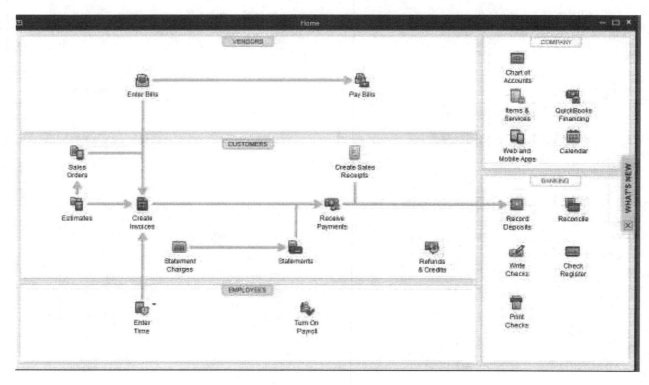

Next review Company Preferences found under Edit/Preferences.

Our accounting year is 1/1/2013 to 12/31/2013. Under Accounting: "Uncheck" Warn if transactions are 90 days in the past:

Also set closing date: 12/31/2012. This indicates that the books have been closed as of that date and we will be accounting for 2013 transactions.

Under Items & Inventory: check the box: Inventory and purchase orders are active.

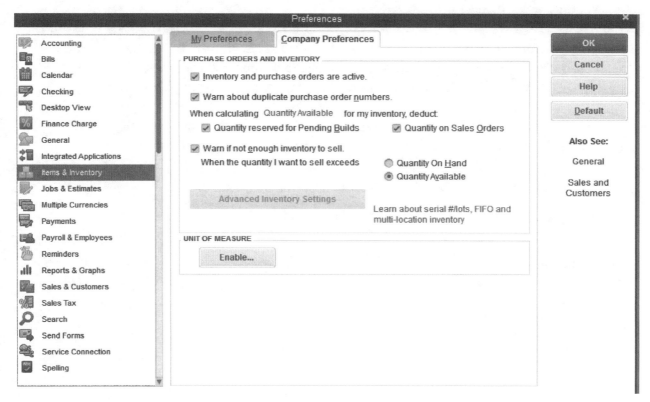

Under Sales & Customers: enter "add new" usual shipping method: Hand deliver

Other General Information:

- Maintain customers and vendors as needed, entering only basic information as indicated. Residential customers will have credit terms of n/10, and commercial customers credit terms of 2/10, n/30 from **statement date**. Use invoice numbering as assigned: Invoice # 1, 2, 3....   Dave will review, approve and initial all customer and vendor credit/debit memos. Vendors are corporations (non-1099) unless otherwise noted.

- Cash-related: Make deposits as checks are received each month. Take advantage of cash discounts whenever possible. Dave Michaels must also sign any checks over $1,000. <u>Dave will review the quarterly check register for reasonableness and initial.</u>

- Maintain inventory items as needed; use perpetual inventory system using average costing. Account for discounts through separate purchase discount account.

- Use expense method to account for supplies.

January, 2013 Transactions/Activities

#1: Using a general journal, T-accounts, and a 2-column form (found on the following pages), **MANUALLY** journalize the five January transactions (1/5 – 1/24), post to the T-accounts (create as needed), and prepare a trial balance.

#2: Account for the following transactions using QuickBooks. Note: we will <u>add</u> accounts as needed here for each transaction. At this time, edit the following accounts:

Change Owner's Equity to YOUR NAME, Capital

Change Furniture and Equipment to Office Equipment

Change Landscaping Equipment to Lawn and Landscaping Equipment

1/5   Record initial investment by Dave (owner), $30,000, record as a general journal entry.

Pull-down Menu item: Accountant/Make General Journal Entries:

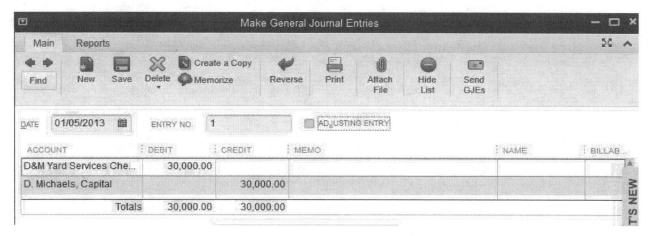

Uncheck adjusting entry box, say "OK" to post entry to Retained Earnings. Note: because this general journal entry is being made directly to the general ledger D & M Yard Services Checking Account, no further deposit is necessary.

1/10 Issued check #1001 to purchase $43 office supplies, $750 computer and $200 printer at Office City, $1,042.65 total includes sales tax (5%). _Use $500 capitalization amount._ (For **THIS** transaction only, allocate sales tax to items; there should not be a sales tax expense, sales tax becomes part of the cost of the item.) Use Write Check from Home Page. At Pay to the Order: Add new vendor. Enter only vendor name and company name (Office City) and Office Supplies Expense under Account Settings to save data entry time. Uncheck Print Later box and enter check number; then the check does not have to be _printed_ to be recorded in the check register.

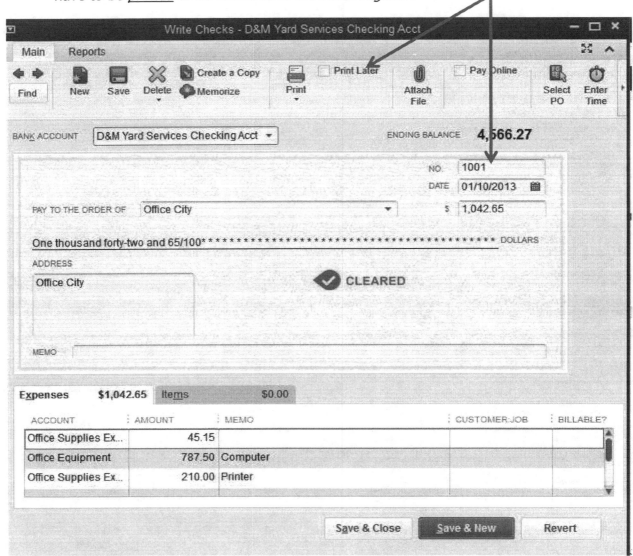

1/15 Bought lawn mower $200, lawn tractor $2500, and trailer $2,000 from PP Equipment, invoice #6908, 6-months free financing, 9% interest charged on unpaid balance after

7/15/2013. *(Note: these amounts **include** sales tax.) Use Enter Bill from Home Page, which will account for this invoice in A/P until partially paid in July. Add new vendor. Add New General Ledger Account for Small Tools and Equipment.*

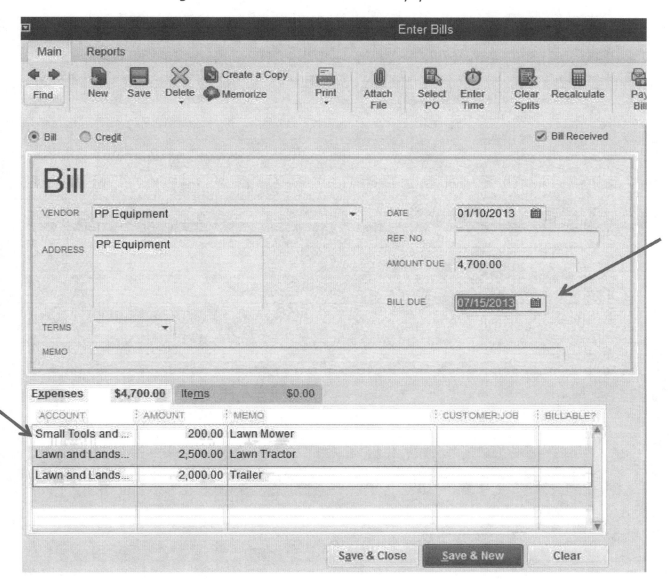

1/16 Dave invested his 2009 Chevy pick-up truck, GVWR (gross vehicle weight rating) is 6250#, into business. Cost was $27,500 when purchased new, estimated fair market value (FMV) at date of investment is $18,200. Truck will be exclusively for business use. *Record at FMV as a general journal entry, add new Truck account.*

1/24 Bought miscellaneous small tools from PP Equipment: 4 shovels $91.96, 2 rakes $29.98, 4 gas cans $159.80, broom $17, total $313.68. All amounts include sales tax. Paid with check #1002. *Write Check.*

1/31 Prepare bank reconciliation for January. *Use Reconcile Icon from Home Page.*

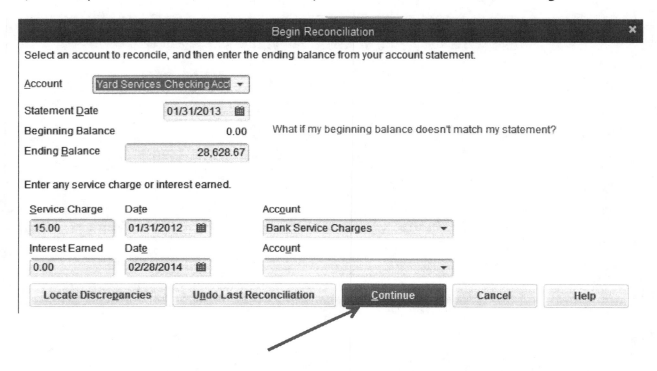

On next screen, check all cleared deposits and checks as noted on the January bank statement.

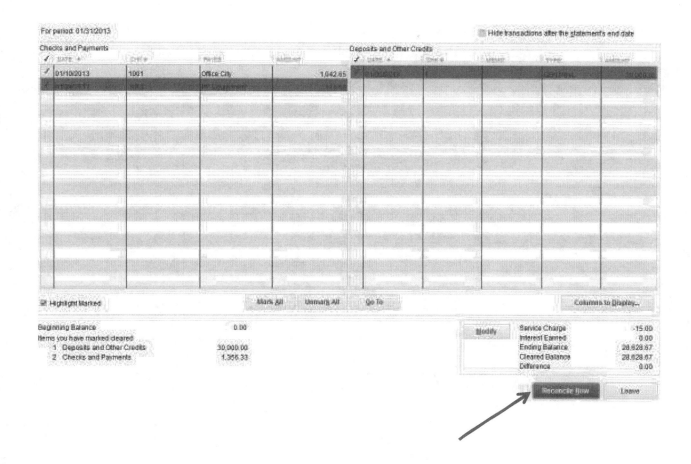

Your January reconciliation detail report should show the following:

D & M Yard Services
Reconciliation Detail
All Transactions

Type	Date	Num	Name	Clr	Amount	Balance
Beginning Balance						0.00
Cleared Transactions						
Checks and Payments - 3 items						
▶ Check	01/10/2013	1001	Office City	✓	-1,042.65	-1,042.65 ◀
Check	01/24/2013	1002	PP Equipment	✓	-313.68	-1,356.33
Check	01/31/2013			✓	-15.00	-1,371.33
Total Checks and Payments					-1,371.33	-1,371.33
Deposits and Credits - 1 item						
General Journal	01/05/2013	1		✓	30,000.00	30,000.00
Total Deposits and Credits					30,000.00	30,000.00
Total Cleared Transactions					28,628.67	28,628.67
Cleared Balance					28,628.67	28,628.67
Register Balance as of 01/31/2013					28,628.67	28,628.67
Ending Balance					28,628.67	28,628.67

To complete January, reconcile (review and make corrections if needed) your trial balance found under Reports/Accountant & Taxes/Trial Balance to the trial balance below:

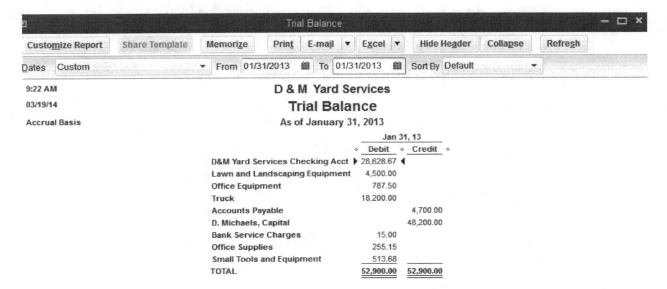

	Trial Balance			– □ ×
Customize Report	Share Template	Memorize	Print	E-mail ▼	Excel ▼	Hide Header	Collapse	Refresh

Dates Custom ▼ From 01/31/2013 🗓 To 01/31/2013 🗓 Sort By Default ▼

9:22 AM
03/19/14
Accrual Basis

D & M Yard Services
Trial Balance
As of January 31, 2013

	Jan 31, 13	
	Debit	Credit
D&M Yard Services Checking Acct	28,628.67	
Lawn and Landscaping Equipment	4,500.00	
Office Equipment	787.50	
Truck	18,200.00	
Accounts Payable		4,700.00
D. Michaels, Capital		48,200.00
Bank Service Charges	15.00	
Office Supplies	255.15	
Small Tools and Equipment	513.68	
TOTAL	**52,900.00**	**52,900.00**

14

XYZ Bank

D & M Yard Services

Acct. # 745-1332   1/1/2013 thru 1/31/2013

Beg. Balance: $0.00

Deposits & CM

1/6 $30,000

Checks & DM

#1001 $1,042.65

#1002   313.68

1/31   SC   15.00

Ending Balance: $28,628.67

January Questions

1. What type of company is D & M Yard Services? Briefly describe the characteristics of a sole-proprietorship, a limited-liability company, and a corporation; specifically address the equity section of the balance sheet for each.

2. Describe the overall objective of internal controls. Identify 3 internal control risks of a landscape business (e.g. theft of assets...), and a possible solution to mitigate those risks (e.g. locks).

3. Discuss the financial statement impact of capitalizing versus expensing costs.

4. On the 1/16 transaction, the FMV was used as the basis to record the transaction. Support this with the *excerpt* from an IRS publication citing this reasoning. (HINT: search on topic: *property changed from personal use)*. Highlight answer.

5. Integrity and ethics are key characteristics of a good accountant; briefly explain how you will address those as you complete this project.

6. Complete: a) Monthly Task List (check off and initial tasks as completed) and b) your To Do/Follow-up Question List with at least two items to be addressed by your "manager"/teacher. (See next page.) You will complete and submit these two items EVERY month.

CHAPTER PRINT/SUBMISSION SUMMARY

1. _____ Manual general journal, T-accounts and trial balance

2. _____ January bank reconciliation detail report prepared in QuickBooks

3. _____ January trial balance (Reports/Accountant & Taxes/Trial Balance)

4. _____ Answers to questions #1 - 5

5. _____ Task List/To Do/Question List (question #6)

Check here if completed	Task	Initials
	Review trial balance for completeness and accuracy	
	Back up your monthly transactions to an external destination (e.g. flash drive), changing file name to the month (e.g. January) 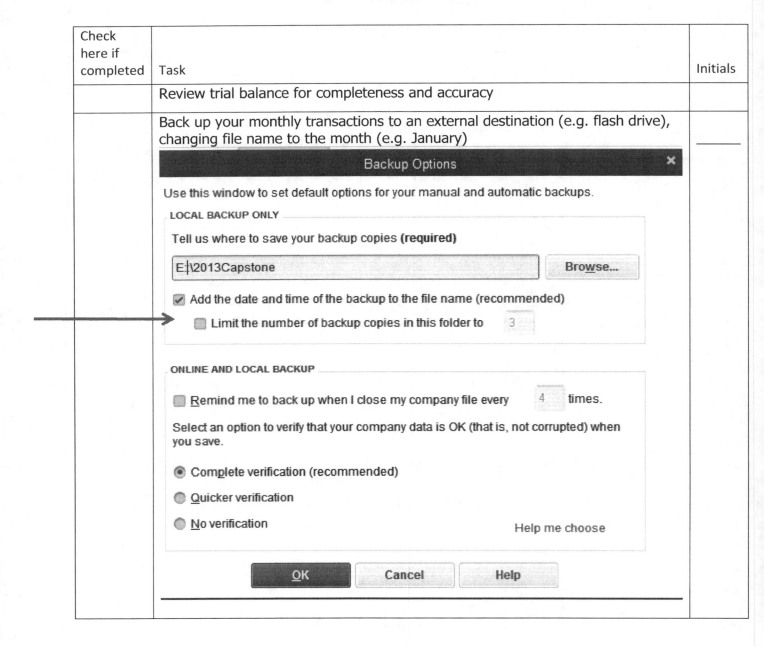	_____

To Do/Follow-up/Question List

February Transactions/Activities

Note: If you are moving between computers, e.g. school and home, you will "Open or restore an Existing Company" from your backup made at the end of January.

2/1   Dave wants to stuff mailboxes with a flyer advertising his services. Prepare a Word document identifying his services:

- Sell, deliver, lay mulch
- Sell, deliver, lay top soil
- Sell and plant small evergreens
- Full lawn maintenance includes spring and fall fertilizing

Use 3 different fonts, WordArt or other tools to enhance advertisement.

2/5   Applied for a WI seller's permit (#789078-5). Print the Business Tax Registration (BTR-101, using any year available) application found on the WI Department of Revenue website. Complete parts A thru F (projecting $3,000 - $5,000 of monthly sales). Also find the WI sales tax publication specific to landscaping services and highlight information specific to D & M Yard Services. Rate = 5%, no county sales tax. *Set-up sales tax QuickBooks: Edit/Preferences/Sales Tax/Company Preferences. QuickBooks will set up a "Tax" item and "Non" taxable item. Add new vendor, WI Dept. of Revenue, and new account, Sales Tax Payable. We will pay sales tax QUARTERLY (when do we pay sales tax?). We will make all existing customers, non-inventory and inventory items taxable at this time. Note: we will have non-taxable customers and will indicate their sales tax setting when we enter customer information.*

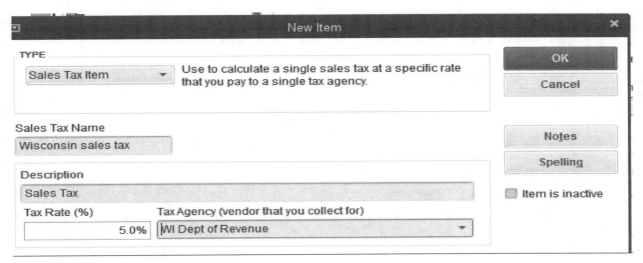

21

2/15   Purchased a string trimmer for $262.50 and a blower for $147 from PP Equipment on the business credit card, total of $409.50. Enter as credit card charge: Banking/Enter Credit Card Charge. Add new account: Type: Credit Card. Account Name: Credit Card Payable.

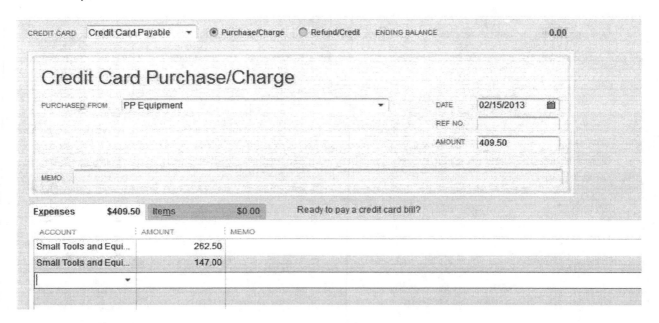

2/17   Signed a 1-year service contract with Cell World. Terms of the contract include a $100 initial set-up fee for two phones, with cost for usage at $60 per month. One phone is for Dave (262-555-3535) for business and one for his wife, Sue, for personal use. All charges will be automatically billed to credit card, and *will be recorded upon receipt* of credit card statement each month. Nothing to be recorded at this time.

2/20   Dave ordered the following from JS Garden Supply on purchase order #1, enter P.O. from Home Page:

- 100 cubic yards of screened topsoil at 17.50/yard (cost)
- 100 cubic yards of mulch at 38.50/yard
- 10 50# bags of grass seed at 48.13/bag
- 10 50# bags of fertilizer at 14.95/bag
- 10 bales of straw at $6/bale
- 12 36" arbor vitae, at $12 each
- 5 5' arbor vitae, $25 each
- 10 2' boxwood bushes at $12.95 each

Add new inventory items for the above items as you complete the purchase order; use retail prices as shown on Suggested Retail Price List on next pages. Add new accounts as necessary, creating a new income account for each item with the exception of straw, combine this with Seeding Income (straw is used when seeding a lawn). See chart of accounts at end of February transactions. All items are taxable. When complete with the purchase order, also enter services (lawn cutting, landscaping labor and snowplowing) as items shown on the retail price list.

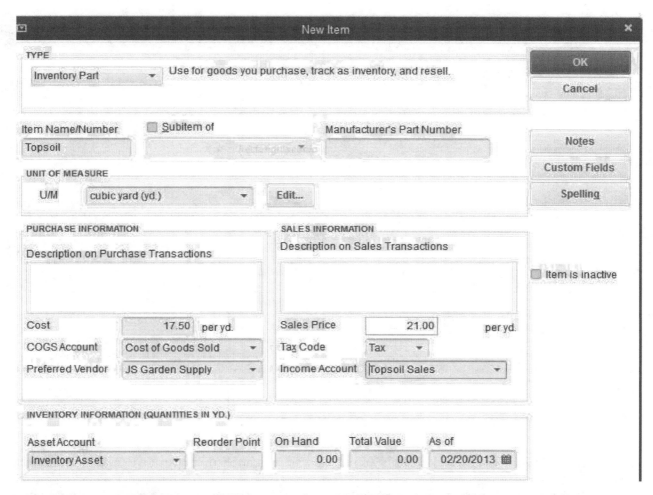

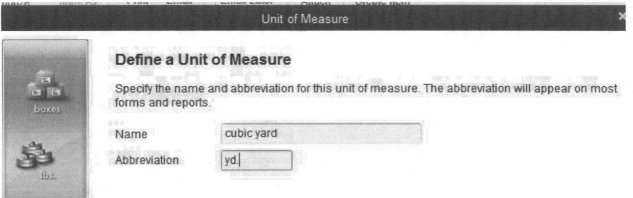

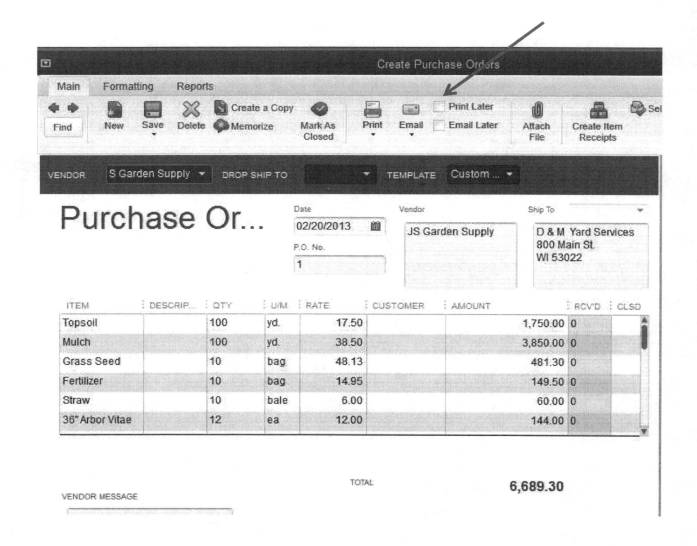

2/22   Filled gas cans, charged $75 on business credit card. *Enter as a credit card charge; adding new vendor: Gas To Go and charging to Auto and Truck Expenses.* All future gas charges are business-related.

2/25   Purchased Microsoft Office and other miscellaneous office supplies at Office City, $387.45; issued check #1003. *Use Write Check.*

2/27   Establish a petty cash fund of $200, check #1004. *Use Write Check, add "Cash" as new vendor and create petty cash account.*

2/28   Dave took draw of $1,000, check #1005. *Use Write Check, add "Your Name" as new vendor and create drawing account.*

2/29   Reconcile cash account for February.

To complete February:

> Review/compare chart of accounts, editing as necessary. Note the separate income and cost of goods sold accounts to facilitate profit analysis of each area of this new business.

Account	Type
D & M Yard Services Checking Acct	Bank
Petty Cash	Bank
Inventory Asset	Other Current Asset
Accumulated Depreciation	Fixed Asset
Lawn and Landscaping Equipment	Fixed Asset
Office Equipment	Fixed Asset
Truck	Fixed Asset
Accounts Payable	Accounts Payable
Credit Card Payable	Credit Card
*Sales Tax Payable	Other Current Liability
Payroll Liabilities	Other Current Liability
Sales Tax Payable	Other Current Liability
D. Michaels, Capital	Equity
D. Michaels, Drawing	Equity
Opening Balance Equity	Equity
Fertilizing Income	Income
Installation Services	Income
Landscaping Services	Income
Lawn Cutting & Trimming	Income
Maintenance Services	Income
Mulch Sales	Income
Nursery Stock Income	Income
Seeding Income	Income
Snowplowing	Income
Topsoil Sales	Income
Cost of Goods Sold	Cost of Goods Sold
Fertilizing Costs	Cost of Goods Sold
Materials Costs	Cost of Goods Sold

Mulch Costs	Cost of Goods Sold
Nursery Stock Cost	Cost of Goods Sold
Seeding Costs	Cost of Goods Sold
Topsoil Costs	Cost of Goods Sold
Advertising and Promotion	Expense
Auto and Truck Expenses	Expense
Bank Service Charges	Expense
Depreciation Expense	Expense
Insurance Expense	Expense
Interest Expense	Expense
Meals and Entertainment	Expense
Office Supplies	Expense
Payroll Expenses	Expense
Postage and Delivery	Expense
Professional Fees	Expense
Rent Expense	Expense
Repairs and Maintenance	Expense
Small Tools and Equipment	Expense
Telephone Expense	Expense
Travel Expense	Expense
Utilities	Expense
Purchase Orders	Non-Posting

➢ Reconcile (review and make corrections if needed) your trial balance found under Reports/Accountant & Taxes/Trial Balance to the trial balance below, noting accounts:

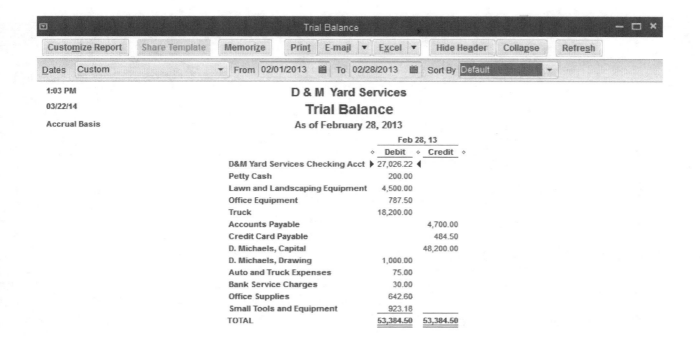

Customize Report | Share Template | Memorize | Print | E-mail ▼ | Excel ▼ | Hide Header | Collapse | Refresh

Dates | Custom ▼ | From 02/01/2013 📅 To 02/28/2013 📅 Sort By Default ▼

1:03 PM

03/22/14

Accrual Basis

D & M Yard Services
Trial Balance
As of February 28, 2013

	Feb 28, 13	
	Debit	Credit
D&M Yard Services Checking Acct	27,026.22	
Petty Cash	200.00	
Lawn and Landscaping Equipment	4,500.00	
Office Equipment	787.50	
Truck	18,200.00	
Accounts Payable		4,700.00
Credit Card Payable		484.50
D. Michaels, Capital		48,200.00
D. Michaels, Drawing	1,000.00	
Auto and Truck Expenses	75.00	
Bank Service Charges	30.00	
Office Supplies	642.60	
Small Tools and Equipment	923.18	
TOTAL	53,384.50	53,384.50

Suggested Retail Price List

Mulch	$46/cubic yard delivered
Screened topsoil	$21/cubic yard delivered
Grass seed	$55/50# bag
Fertilizer	$18/50# bag
Straw	$8/bale
Arbor Vitae 36"	$17.95 each
Arbor Vitae 5'	$30.00 each
Boxwood Bushes	$24.95 each

Lawn cutting and trimming	$35/hour
Labor on landscaping services	$35/hour
Snow plowing	$45/hour

XYZ Bank

D & M Yard Services

Acct. # 745-1332

2/1/2013 thru 2/28/2013

Beg. Balance: $28,628.67

Deposits & CM

Checks & DM

#1004	$ 200.00
#1005	1,000.00
2/28 SC	15.00

Ending Balance: $27,413.67

February Questions

1. Sales tax related:
    a. Determine which services/items of D & M Yard Services are subject to WI sales tax, support by printed resource found on the 2/5 transaction.
    b. List 3 county sales tax rates. Why are they different?
    c. List 1 type of organization exempt from sales tax.
    d. Print the QuickBooks Help screen on how to set up sales tax.

2. Explain the use of purchase orders as a measure of internal control.

3. Set up an Excel or Word petty cash sheet to account for fund activity throughout year. The account will be replenished at year-end. This task is noted in your February task list.

4. Complete: a) Monthly Task List and b) your To Do/Follow-up Question List with at least two items to be addressed by your "manager"/teacher. (See next page.)

CHAPTER PRINT/SUBMISSION SUMMARY

1._____ Advertising flyer

2._____ Seller's permit application (BTR-101)

3._____ February bank reconciliation detail report prepared in QuickBooks

4._____ February trial balance

5._____ Questions #1 - 3

6._____ Task List/To Do/Question List

FEBRUARY TASK LIST

Check here if completed	Task	Initials
	Set up sales tax	
	Set up inventory items	
	Set up sheet (may use Excel or Word) to account for petty cash	
	Set up and review chart of accounts	
	Verify cash balance on trial balance equals cash balance on bank reconciliation	
	Review trial balance for completeness and accuracy	
	Back up your monthly transactions to an external destination (e.g. flash drive), changing file name to the month	

To Do/Follow-up/Question List

March Transactions/Activities

3/2   Received 3 calls from our advertising flyers for mulching jobs. Visited jobs and prepared **estimates**:

Walter Brown: 5 yards, delivered and spread, estimated 2 hours of landscaping services

Davidson Foods: 12 yards, delivered and spread, 6 hours

Forest Hill School (*non-profit, exempt from sales tax/commercial*): 20 yards delivered and spread, 16 hours

Note 1: Add new customers as entering estimates:

<u>Address Info</u>: enter customer name and company name (same)

<u>Payment Settings</u>: Residential will have terms of n/10, statement date (add new) and commercial 2/10, n/30 **from statement date** (add new).   **Note:** Our terms are tailored to our landscape company because in the upcoming months, there will be several services rendered each month to our customers; they would not be expected to pay each invoice, rather a single amount from their monthly statement. The statement date is used because of multiple billings/invoices during the month to your customers; you would not have them pay each invoice; they would pay from the monthly statement.

<u>Sales Tax</u>: All customers are taxable unless otherwise noted.

<u>Additional Info</u>: Add new customer type: residential or commercial

> ➢ Print or PDF Walter Brown's estimate (as shown).

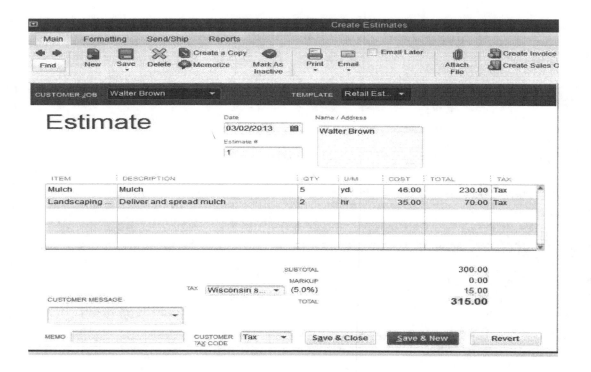

3/3 Signed a 5 year lease to rent 2 acres with garage and heated office space at 900 Main Street for $750 per month from John Smith. Pay security deposit of $1000 and March rent, check #1006. Write check, add new vendor, check the box on tax settings for vendor eligible for 1099 with vendor tax id: 777-77-7777; add other asset account for security deposit. Update company address information.

3/4 Had shelves and counters installed in office and garage. Received invoice from Tom George, carpenter. See document on following pages. Note: remember capitalization limit! *Enter bill, add accounts as needed.*

3/5 Hired Mary Martin (address: 100 Main St., Landscape, WI 53022, regular employee, Social Security #775-13-2222) as part-time office manager at $8/hour. She is single claiming 1 allowance for both federal and state withholding and is subject to Medicare, Social Security, Federal and State Unemployment. Also added Max Smith (address: 200 Main St., Landscape, WI 53022, SS#489-78-1234, Married-3 allowances) part-time/full-time as seasonal lawn care requires, $9.50/hour, time and one-half for overtime hours; both will start 4/2.

> ➢ NOTE 1: The monthly payroll will be paid by check on the last day of each month, starting on 4/30/2013. D & M Yard Services will be a quarterly depositor of 941 taxes (FEIN - federal employer identification number: 39-1212121), state withholding (identification #: 036-3456789012-04) and

state unemployment tax of 4.1% (account #: 876543-211-1). Federal unemployment tax will be paid as required.

> NOTE 2: For this project we will <u>not</u> subscribe to the QuickBooks Payroll Tax Service and will process our payroll manually calculating/inputting the employee withholdings and employer payroll taxes. In QuickBooks Help/ Search: "process payroll manually" and follow below:

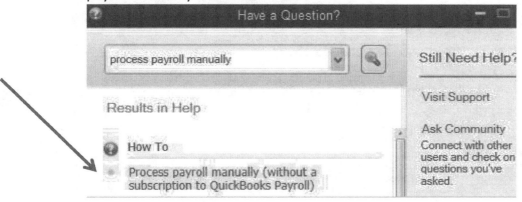

Process payroll manually (without a subscription to QuickBooks Payroll)

What we recommend

We strongly recommend that you sign up for QuickBooks Payroll to make sure that you have the most current tax tables available. In addition to providing current tax tables, QuickBooks Payroll provides additional features that take the worry out of doing your payroll.

If you prefer to process your payroll manually

1. Set your company file to use the manual payroll calculations setting.

"OK"

Home Page should now show:

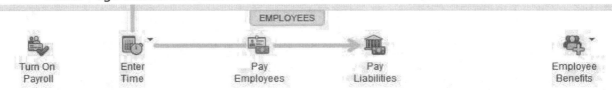

Next: go to Employees menu option/Payroll Setup/Continue

Compensation: Check Salary and Hourly Wage & Overtime Only; then delete Double-time hourly and Bonus/Continue

We will set up employee benefits in July

Next: Employee Setup

Next: Taxes; use information above.

NOTE 3: The default is to account for all employee withholdings and employer tax liabilities in ONE account: Payroll Liabilities; we will edit this later.

* State Tax	Description
WI - Withholding	State Income/Withholding Tax
WI - Unemployment	4.1%

Review your Scheduled Tax Payments list

* Scheduled Payments	Description
Federal 940	Check\Quarterly (usual frequency)
Federal 941/944/943	Check\Quarterly
WI Unemployment Insurance	Check\Quarterly (usual frequency)
WI Withholding	Check\Quarterly

3/5 Received monthly credit card statement (see statement on next pages). Right click on "Credit Card Payable", use register to <u>compare</u> charges already recorded to the <u>March statement</u>. Record any additional charges not previously recorded using the statement date. Purchases from any food store or drug store are personal expenses and should be charged to the drawing account. See document.

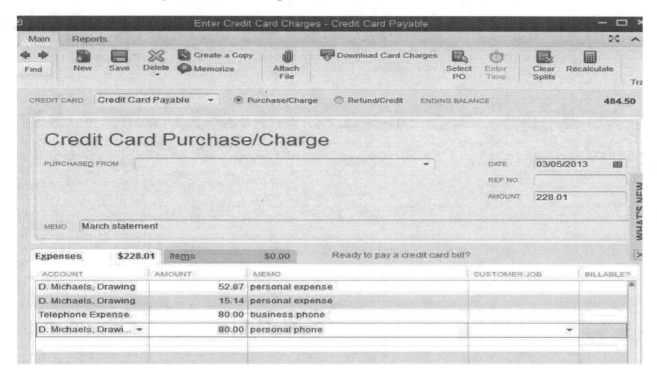

After saving, note updated ending balance which agrees with credit card statement:

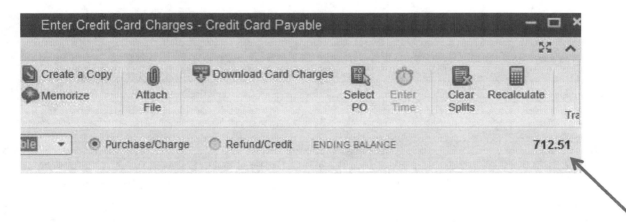

3/7 Received items ordered from JS Garden Supply. There were no boxwood bushes available. Invoice #475 received with terms 2/10, n/30; set vendor terms before receiving inventory with bill. Verify that total amount due does not include amounts for boxwood bushes.

3/12 Delivered and spread mulch at Davidson Foods. Converted sales estimate to invoice, use default invoice number; it is ok to leave "Print Later" box checked.

Customize invoice. Use "Formatting" tab to Customize Data Layout. Delete the following fields: P.O. No., REP, FOB and Project/Job fields from screen and print. Then use Layout Designer to move Terms boxes over next to Ship Date and name your invoice template.

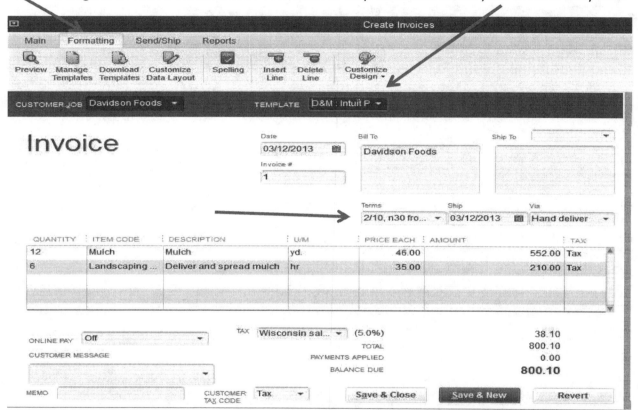

3/13 Record charged gas of $52. (Although this will be on the April credit card statement, record at this time.)

3/15 Dave approved payment of March credit card statement; on *enter credit card charges* screen, select "Ready to pay a credit card bill?" and follow help instructions to reconcile to March statement and pay only the amount owed on March statement (check #1007). Add new vendor: Credit Card Services, Inc. and payment settings/terms of net 10. Dave also reviewed A/P Aging Detail as of 3/15/2013; paying open invoices for JS Garden Supply (set discount, charging to new account: Purchase Discounts; type: Cost of Goods Sold) and Tom George, checks #1008 – 1009.

3/17   Contracted with the following customers for seasonal lawn maintenance which includes cutting and trimming:

-Walter Brown	2 hours
-Joe Calhoun	3 hours
-Forest Hill School	4 hours
-Jacksonville Industrial Park	6 hours
-Larry Laxson	2 hours
-Paul Garrett	3 hours
-Nottingham Condominium Complex	8 hours

Prepare **sales orders** for these customers. Add new customers as needed (See March 2 for detailed instructions for adding customers).

3/20   Record charged gas of $68.

3/22   Completed estimated mulch work at Forest Hill School. Create invoice.

3/26   Arranged for utility budget billing of $150 per month for office gas and electric with Utility Service Corp.; charged to business credit card, record. (Note: it is not necessary to set up a vendor for these charges.)

3/31   Dave reviewed the Unpaid Bills Detail report (Vendors & Payables); authorizing payments for any invoices **due**.

3/31   Dave withdrew $500, check #1010.

3/31   Prepare customized customer statements for March. Go to Lists/Templates/select Intuit Standard Statement. Manage template. Copy, then change template name to "Your Name" Yard Services. Select Additional Customization on the bottom of screen.

Select Footer, check box and enter text as seen in the screen shot below. Accept changes, "OK", use default layout, "Yes"….

This ONE custom message is being tailored to _our_ company due to the different residential and commercial customer types.

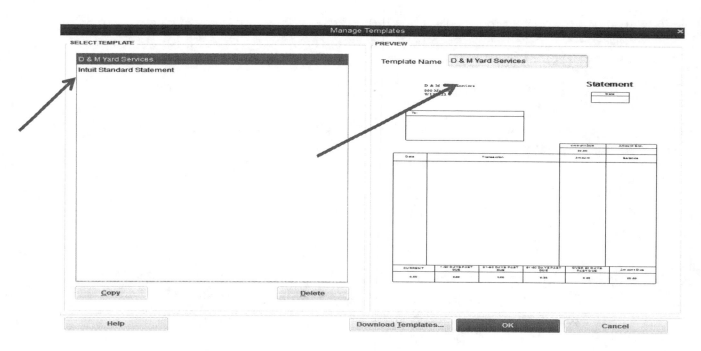

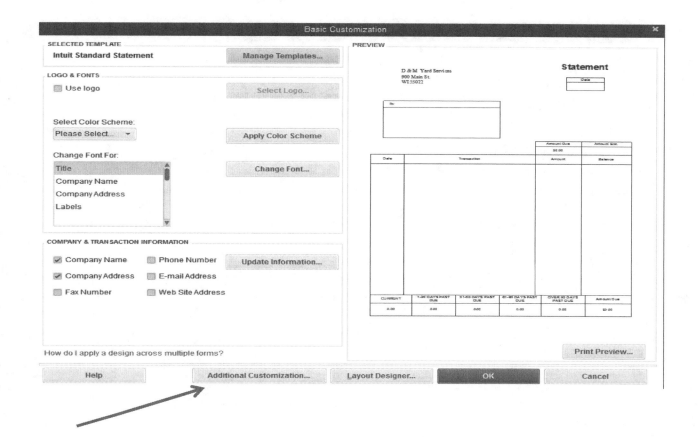

How do I apply a design across multiple forms?

Help   Additional Customization...   Layout Designer...   OK   Cancel

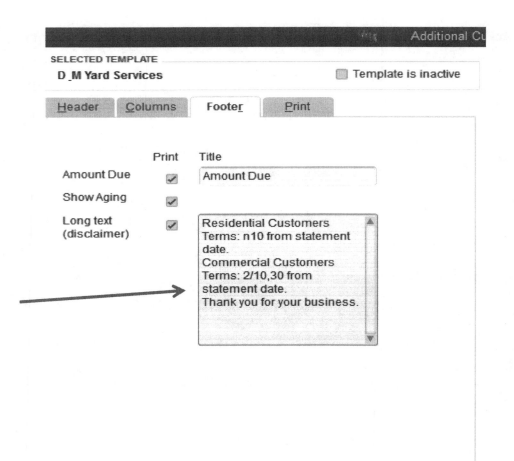

In your template list you should now see a "D & M" Yard Services template as seen below:

D & M Yard Services	Statement

> Prepare statements for Davidson Foods and Forest Hill School; print to PDF file for submission.

3/31   Reconcile cash account for March (Note: You would inquire on old outstanding checks) and compare (review and make corrections if needed) your trial balance found under Reports/Accountant & Taxes/Trial Balance to the following reports.

D & M Yard Services
Reconciliation Detail
D&M Yard Services Checking Acct, Period Ending 03/31/2013

Type	Date	Num	Name	Clr	Amount	Balance
Beginning Balance						27,413.67
Cleared Transactions						
Checks and Payments - 4 items						
Check	03/03/2013	1006	John Smith	X	-1,750.00	-1,750.00
Bill Pmt - Check	03/15/2013	1008	JS Garden Supply	X	-6,428.60	-8,178.60
Check	03/15/2013	1007	Credit Card Service...	X	-712.51	-8,891.11
Check	03/31/2013			X	-15.00	-8,906.11
Total Checks and Payments					-8,906.11	-8,906.11
Total Cleared Transactions					-8,906.11	-8,906.11
Cleared Balance					-8,906.11	18,507.56
Uncleared Transactions						
Checks and Payments - 3 items						
Check	02/25/2013	1003	Office City		-387.45	-387.45
Bill Pmt - Check	03/15/2013	1009	Tom George		-850.00	-1,237.45
Check	03/31/2013	1010	Dave Michaels		-500.00	-1,737.45
Total Checks and Payments					-1,737.45	-1,737.45
Total Uncleared Transactions					-1,737.45	-1,737.45
Register Balance as of 03/31/2013					-10,643.56	16,770.11
New Transactions						
Checks and Payments - 7 items						
Check	04/01/2013	1011	John Smith		-750.00	-750.00
Check	04/07/2013	1012	American Insurance		-1,410.00	-2,160.00
Check	04/15/2013	1015	IRS		-500.00	-2,660.00
Check	04/15/2013	1014	Credit Card Service...		-342.80	-3,002.80
Check	04/15/2013	1016	WI Dept of Revenue		-150.00	-3,152.80
Bill Pmt - Check	04/15/2013	1013	JS Garden Supply		-126.91	-3,279.71
Paycheck	04/30/2013	1017	Mary Martin		-303.58	-3,583.29
Total Checks and Payments					-3,583.29	-3,583.29
Total New Transactions					-3,583.29	-3,583.29
Ending Balance					-14,226.85	13,186.82

D & M Yard Services
Trial Balance
As of March 31, 2013

	Mar 31, 13	
	Debit	Credit
D&M Yard Services Checking Acct	16,770.11	
Petty Cash	200.00	
Accounts Receivable	2,280.10	
Inventory Asset	5,327.80	
Lawn and Landscaping Equipment	4,500.00	
Office Equipment	787.50	
Truck	18,200.00	
Leasehold Improvements	850.00	
Security Deposit	1,000.00	
Accounts Payable		4,700.00
Credit Card Payable		270.00
Sales Tax Payable		38.10
D. Michaels, Capital		48,200.00
D. Michaels, Drawing	1,648.01	
Landscaping Services		770.00
Mulch Sales		1,472.00
Mulch Costs	1,232.00	
Purchase Discounts		131.20
Auto and Truck Expenses	195.00	
Bank Service Charges	45.00	
Office Supplies	642.60	
Rent Expense	750.00	
Small Tools and Equipment	923.18	
Telephone Expense	80.00	
Utilities	150.00	
TOTAL	55,581.30	55,581.30

Tom George Carpenter

INVOICE

Address	500 Main St.
City, State, ZIP	Pewaukee, WI 53072
	39-4568791
	(sole-proprietor)

SOLD TO:

Name	D & M Yard Services
Address	900 Main St.
City, State, ZIP	Landscape, WI 53022

INVOICE NUMBER	536524
INVOICE DATE	March 4, 2013
TERMS	Net 15

DESCRIPTION	AMOUNT
Installed shelves and counter in office and garage	$650.00
Materials	200.00
	$850.00 PAY THIS AMOUNT

THANK YOU FOR YOUR BUSINESS!

Credit Card Services, Inc.

D & M Yard Services

Statement Date: 3/5/2013

Use month as invoice number

Amount Due: 712.51

Due Date: 3/15/2013

Charge Summary:

Date	Merchant	Amount
2/15	ABC Food Store	52.87
2/15	PP Equipment	409.50
2/18	Max's Drug Store	15.14
2/17	Cell World	160.00
2/22	Gas To Go	75.00

XYZ Bank

D & M Yard Services

Acct. # 745-1332   3/1/2013 thru 3/31/2013

Beg. Balance: 27413.67

Deposits & CM

Checks & DM

#1006   1750.00

#1007   712.51

#1008   6428.60

3/31   SC   15.00

Ending Balance: $ 18507.56

March Questions

1. It is noted that the business credit card is used for business and personal expenses; list the business and personal expenses for March. Address the *accounting* and *ethical* reason for this separation of expenses.

2. Dave Michaels takes advantage of cash discounts whenever possible. Address the business reason for this decision. Address the *ethical* ramifications if Dave would take the discount when paying outside the discount period.

3. Support the accounting for the installation of shelves and counters as a leasehold improvement. (No specific source.)

4. Verify the A/R, Inventory & A/P control account balances per the trial balance agree with one of the respective (A/R, Inventory or A/P) detail reports; document this in your Word document started above in question #1.

   Example: A/R balance per trial balance   = _____

              A/R sub. ledger bal. per A/R _____(report name) = _____

   QuickBooks has many reports; review the variety of reports in the different areas, e.g. Company & Financial, Customers & Receivables...

5. As a measure of internal control over sequentially numbered invoices through March 31, prepare report of numerically sorted invoices from the Customer Center/Transactions/Invoice (see bottom of screen for report).

6. Complete: a) Monthly Task List and b) your To Do/Follow-up Question List with at least two items to be addressed by your "manager"/teacher.

7. Prepare a short presentation addressing 2 managerial/business-related (e.g. internal controls, marketing...) and 3 financial-related items. Submit a presentation outline. Note: instructor will select students each quarter.

CHAPTER PRINT/SUBMISSION SUMMARY

NOTE: This month's print/submissions include various reports as an example of reports in these areas, i.e. sales/customers, vendors/payables... These will <u>not</u> all be printed each month! Also, note all reports can be converted into Excel or PDF file(via print) on the report window.

1._____ Walter Brown's estimate

2._____ Davidson Foods invoice (using customized invoice template)

3._____ Davidson Foods and Forest Hill School customer statements

4._____ Report to support A/R subsidiary ledger balance (question #4). Note: there is more than one possible report

5._____ Report to support A/P subsidiary ledger balance (question #4)

6._____ Report to support Inventory subsidiary ledger balance (question #4)

7._____ Report of numerically sorted invoices for quarter

8._____ Check Detail for January – March (initialed by Dave to indicate review for the quarter)

9._____ Bank Account Detail Reconciliation Report

10._____Trial Balance

11.____ Questions #1 – 4

12.____ Task List/To Do/ Question List

13. ____ Outline of presentation for selected students

MARCH TASK LIST

Check here if completed	Task	Initials
	Review of Unpaid Bills Detail Report at March 15 and 31	
	Compare A/R control account balance (A/R on trial balance) to a detail report of the A/R subsidiary ledger	
	Compare A/P control account balance (A/P on trial balance) to a detail report of the A/P subsidiary ledger	
	Compare Inventory control account balance (Inventory on trial balance) to a detail report of the Inventory subsidiary ledger	
	Prepare report of numerically sorted invoices from the Customer Center/Transactions/Invoice	
	Review check detail for January – March, Dave indicates review with his initials on report (see cash-related information at beginning of project) Export report into Excel to note initials.	
	Review general ledger for January – March (NOTE: on screen ONLY; no printing)	
	Verify cash balance on trial balance equals cash balance on bank reconciliation	
	Review trial balance for completeness and accuracy	
	Back up your monthly transactions to an external destination (e.g. flash drive), changing file name to the month	

To Do/Follow-up/Question List

April Transactions/Activities

NOTE 1: Enter check numbers when preparing checks to avoid printing checks; remember to uncheck "print later" box.

NOTE 2: Since you have now completed the first quarter of transactions, fewer instructions will be provided. Add customers, vendors and accounts as needed. Use QuickBooks Help when needed.

4/1   Paid monthly rent, check #1011; *memorize* this transaction. We will "Add to my Reminders List" versus automating the entry so the check number can be entered each month.

4/2   Mary and Max started today; payroll will be paid at the end of each month.

4/2   Bought a small refrigerator for the office for $30.45 on the credit card. Record. A vendor is not required.

4/2   Completed Brown's mulch job. Create invoice from estimate. *(Reminder: customers will pay from their monthly statements which we will prepare at the end of each month; WATCH commercial customer discounts! Because of using 2/10 from STATEMENT DATE, you may have to input discount!)*

4/3   Used $7.86 of petty cash to buy water and soda for office. Account for these on your petty cash sheet.

4/3   Received payments in full from Davidson Foods and Forest Hill School. WATCH DISCOUNTS – YOU WILL HAVE TO CALCULATE AND ENTER USING DISCOUNTS AND CREDITS ICON! Also Record Deposit as of date received.

4/5   Bought office paper and printer ink from Office City, charged credit card $36.42, record.

4/5   Received credit card statement. Reconcile credit card payable to April statement balance noting difference, enter any additional charges, return to reconciliation to check off new charges, difference should equal zero.

        Reminders:
> All gas charges on credit card are for the business only.
> Cell World bill is for Dave's business phone and his wife's personal phone.
> ABC Food Store, Deli Stop... are personal charges.
> Utility Service Corp. is a business charge.

4/7   Paid $960 and $450 to American Insurance for 6 months, April – September, for workers compensation (comp) and business owner's insurance respectively, check #1012. Charge the entire amount to unexpired insurance. *Make a general journal entry as of 4/30/2013 to record the expiration of April insurance, then memorize the transaction and Automate Transaction Entry to recur for the next 5 months, both types of insurance may be charged to Insurance Expense. [See the following screen shot]*

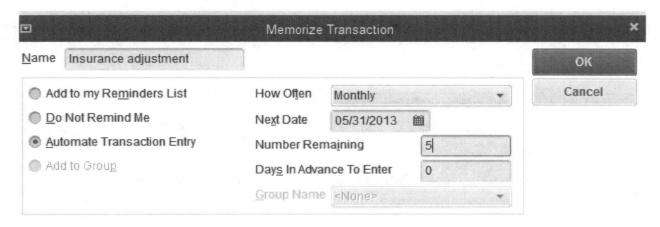

4/8 Boxwood bushes from JS Garden Supply were delivered. Invoice #782, terms from original order still apply.

4/10 Applied spring fertilizer for customers:

Brown: 1 bag/1hour of landscaping labor

Calhoun: 1 bag/1hour

Forest Hill School: 4 bags/2 hours

Jacksonville Industrial Park: 4 bags/2 hours

Create *new* invoices (these are not from estimates or orders), noting customers will receive statements at month-end and pay from statements.

4/15 Dave reviewed A/P Aging Detail and approved payment to JS Garden Supply, as well as payment due to Credit Card Services (pay a credit card bill), checks #1013 and 1014. Watch discounts. Assign check numbers.

4/15 Picked-up 10 bags of fertilizer from JS Garden Supply, invoice #841. <u>No</u> discount given on small orders.

4/15 Paid quarterly income tax estimates, $500 federal, $150 Wisconsin. *Set-up vendor account to IRS; <u>WI</u> Dept. of Revenue is already added from sales tax; it is ok to use that vendor account (the <u>Wisconsin</u> Dept. of Revenue vendor was added during the payroll set up process, we will use that vendor for our state withholding payments); print forms for estimates (<u>IRS</u> 1040-ES and <u>WI</u> 1-ES) and write checks #1015 and 1016 respectively. Social Security number for Dave's wife, Sue, is 360-24-9781. Note: D & M Yard Services is a sole-proprietorship for which the income will be reported on Dave and*

Sue's federal & state income tax returns; these deposits should be properly charged to drawing. Save forms for future estimates.

4/21   Applied spring fertilizing and seeding for customers:

Laxson: 1 bag/1 hour of landscaping services

Garrett: 1 bag/1 hour

Nottingham Condos: 6 bags/3 hours; also spread 2 bags of grass seed, using 3 straw bales and an additional 2 hours.

Create new invoices.

4/27   Completed lawn maintenance for ALL contracted customers. Create invoices from March 17th sales orders. After completing EACH invoice, SAVE using icon to top of invoice icon bar, remove invoice and sales order number (S. O. No.) and memorize invoice for future use. Do not record invoices with changes of deleted invoice and sales order number. *Next month to invoice monthly customers, go to Lists, Memorized Transaction List, select transaction, edit date and save – watch dates!*

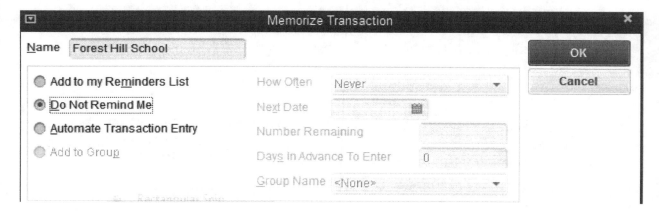

4/30   Prepare monthly payroll:

Mary: 42 hours (ck. #1017)   Max: 80 hours (ck. #1018)

Reminder: we will not be using a QuickBooks payroll service to calculate payroll withholdings and taxes.

From the payroll setup information you entered in March, your Employees/Manage Payroll Items/View/Edit Payroll Item List should have the following deductions and employer taxes set up:

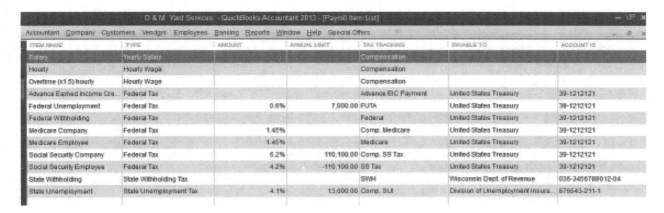

ITEM NAME	TYPE	AMOUNT	ANNUAL LIMIT	TAX TRACKING	PAYABLE TO	ACCOUNT ID
Salary	Yearly Salary			Compensation		
Hourly	Hourly Wage			Compensation		
Overtime (x1.5) hourly	Hourly Wage			Compensation		
Advance Earned Income Cre...	Federal Tax			Advance EIC Payment	United States Treasury	39-1212121
Federal Unemployment	Federal Tax	0.6%	7,000.00	FUTA	United States Treasury	39-1212121
Federal Withholding	Federal Tax			Federal	United States Treasury	39-1212121
Medicare Company	Federal Tax	1.45%		Comp. Medicare	United States Treasury	39-1212121
Medicare Employee	Federal Tax	1.45%		Medicare	United States Treasury	39-1212121
Social Security Company	Federal Tax	6.2%	110,100.00	Comp. SS Tax	United States Treasury	39-1212121
Social Security Employee	Federal Tax	4.2%	-110,100.00	SS Tax	United States Treasury	39-1212121
State Withholding	State Withholding Tax			SWH	Wisconsin Dept. of Revenue	036-3456789012-04
State Unemployment	State Unemployment Tax	4.1%	13,000.00	Comp. SUI	Division of Unemployment Insura...	676543-211-1

We will make each payroll item from Advanced Earned Income Credit to State Unemployment INACTIVE and add new deductions and company contributions.

Right click on each item: Make Payroll Item Inactive

On the payroll screen, right click, add new items: DEDUCTIONS or COMPANY CONTRIBUTIONS and ADD new accounts for payables and expenses as noted here (QuickBooks records all liabilities to one account, Payroll Liabilities and all expenses to one account, Payroll Expense; make these accounts INACTIVE).

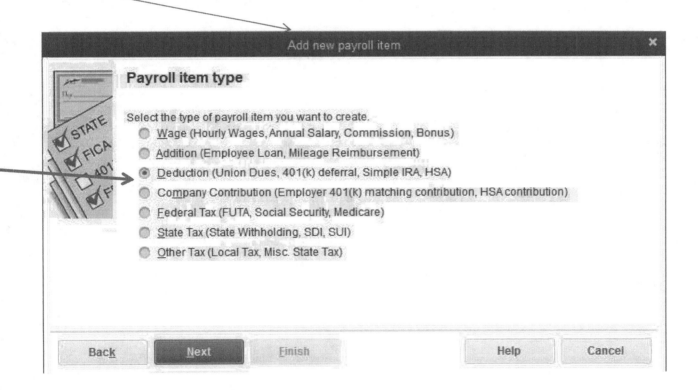

Social Security (deduction): FICA Payable, 6.2%, wage limit of $113,700

St. Withholding: SWT Payable, 2% of gross wages, no wage limit

Social Security-Employer: FICA Payable and FICA Tax Expense, 6.2%, wage limit of $113,700

Advance Earned Income Credit: Not used

Federal Unemployment: FUTA Payable and FUTA Tax Expense, .6%, wage limit of $7,000

Federal Withholding: FIT Payable, no calculation, we will enter this withholding per withholding charts below

Medicare Company: FICA Payable and FICA Tax Expense, 1.45%, no wage limit

Medicare Employee: FICA Payable. 1.45%, no wage limit

State Unemployment: SUTA Payable and SUTA Tax Expense, 4.1%, $13,000 wage limit

Item screen after editing:

ITEM NAME	TYPE	AMOUNT	ANNUAL LIMIT	TAX TRACKING	PAYABLE TO	ACCOUNT ID
Salary	Yearly Salary			Compensation		
Hourly	Hourly Wage			Compensation		
Overtime (x1.5) hourly	Hourly Wage			Compensation		
Fed Withholding	Deduction	0.00		None	United States Treasury	39-1212121
Medicare - Employee	Deduction	-1.45%		None	United States Treasury	39-1212121
Social Security	Deduction	-6.2%	-113,700.00	None	United States Treasury	39-1212121
St. Withholding	Deduction	-2.0%		None	WI Dept of Revenue	3456789012-04
Fed. Unemployment	Company Contribution	0.6%	7,000.00	None	United States Treasury	39-1212121
Medicare - Employer	Company Contribution	1.45%		None	United States Treasury	39-1212121
Social Security - Employer	Company Contribution	6.2%	113,700.00	None	United States Treasury	39-1212121
St. Unemployment	Company Contribution	4.1%	13,000.00	None	WI Dept. of Workforce Development	876543-211-1
Advance Earned Income Cre...	Federal Tax			Advance EIC Payment	United States Treasury	39-1212121

Lastly edit accounts for the salary, hourly and overtime to these expense accounts:

Salary: Office Wages

Hourly: Field Wages

Overtime: Field Wages

Add these earnings, deductions and company contributions to the Employee Defaults:
Employees/right click on an employee/Employee Defaults.

Each employee should show as below:

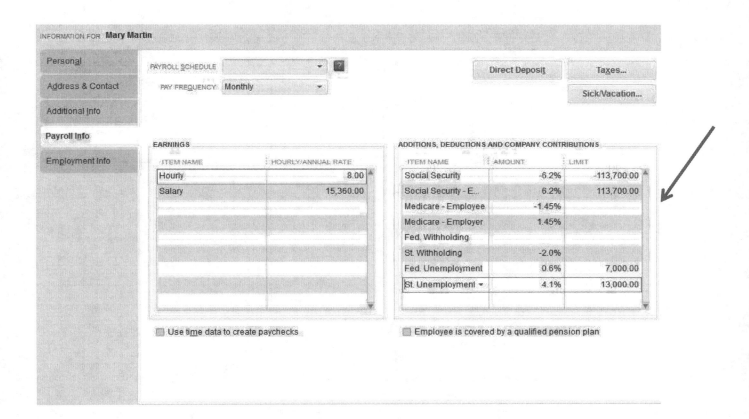

Pay Employees/Enter pay period ending and check dates/"Check" Mary/Open paycheck
detail and deductions and company contributions will calculate; **ENTER** federal
withholding with a minus sign as determined by the following withholding tables. Assign
paycheck numbers manually.

SINGLE Persons—MONTHLY Payroll Period

(For Wages Paid through December 2013)

And the wages are—		And the number of withholding allowances claimed is —										
At least	But less than	0	1	2	3	4	5	6	7	8	9	10
		The amount of income tax to be withheld is—										
$ 0	$ 220	$ 0	$ 0	$ 0	$ 0	$ 0	$ 0	$ 0	$0	$0	$0	$0
220	230	4	0	0	0	0	0	0	0	0	0	0
230	240	5	0	0	0	0	0	0	0	0	0	0
240	250	6	0	0	0	0	0	0	0	0	0	0
250	260	7	0	0	0	0	0	0	0	0	0	0
260	270	8	0	0	0	0	0	0	0	0	0	0
270	280	9	0	0	0	0	0	0				
280	290	10	0	0	0	0	0	0				
290	300	11	0	0	0	0	0	0		MONTHLY SINGLE PERSONS			
300	320	13	0	0	0	0	0	0				
320	340	15	0	0	0	0	0	0				
340	360	17	0	0	0	0	0	0				
360	380	19	0	0	0	0	0	0	0	0	0	0
380	400	21	0	0	0	0	0	0	0	0	0	0
400	420	23	0	0	0	0	0	0	0	0	0	0
420	440	25	0	0	0	0	0	0	0	0	0	0
440	460	27	0	0	0	0	0	0	0	0	0	0
460	480	29	0	0	0	0	0	0	0	0	0	0
480	500	31	0	0	0	0	0	0	0	0	0	0
500	520	33	0	0	0	0	0	0	0	0	0	0
520	540	35	2	0	0	0	0	0	0	0	0	0
540	560	37	4	0	0	0	0	0	0	0	0	0
560	580	39	6	0	0	0	0	0	0	0	0	0
580	600	41	8	0	0	0	0	0	0	0	0	0
600	640	44	11	0	0	0	0	0	0	0	0	0
640	680	48	15	0	0	0	0	0	0	0	0	0
680	720	52	19	0	0	0	0	0	0	0	0	0
720	760	56	23	0	0	0	0	0	0	0	0	0
760	800	60	27	0	0	0	0	0	0	0	0	0
800	840	64	31	0	0	0	0	0	0	0	0	0
840	880	68	35	3	0	0	0	0	0	0	0	0
880	920	72	39	7	0	0	0	0	0	0	0	0
920	960	76	43	11	0	0	0	0	0	0	0	0
960	1,000	82	47	15	0	0	0	0	0	0	0	0
1,000	1,040	88	51	19	0	0	0	0	0	0	0	0
1,040	1,080	94	55	23	0	0	0	0	0	0	0	0
1,080	1,120	100	59	27	0	0	0	0	0	0	0	0
1,120	1,160	106	63	31	0	0	0	0	0	0	0	0
1,160	1,200	112	67	35	2	0	0	0	0	0	0	0
1,200	1,240	118	71	39	6	0	0	0	0	0	0	0
1,240	1,280	124	76	43	10	0	0	0	0	0	0	0
1,280	1,320	130	82	47	14	0	0	0	0	0	0	0
1,320	1,360	136	88	51	18	0	0	0	0	0	0	0
1,360	1,400	142	94	55	22	0	0	0	0	0	0	0
1,400	1,440	148	100	59	26	0	0	0	0	0	0	0
1,440	1,480	154	106	63	30	0	0	0	0	0	0	0
1,480	1,520	160	112	67	34	2	0	0	0	0	0	0
1,520	1,560	166	118	71	38	6	0	0	0	0	0	0
1,560	1,600	172	124	75	42	10	0	0	0	0	0	0
1,600	1,640	178	130	81	46	14	0	0	0	0	0	0
1,640	1,680	184	136	87	50	18	0	0	0	0	0	0
1,680	1,720	190	142	93	54	22	0	0	0	0	0	0
1,720	1,760	196	148	99	58	26	0	0	0	0	0	0
1,760	1,800	202	154	105	62	30	0	0	0	0	0	0
1,800	1,840	208	160	111	66	34	1	0	0	0	0	0
1,840	1,880	214	166	117	70	38	5	0	0	0	0	0
1,880	1,920	220	172	123	74	42	9	0	0	0	0	0
1,920	1,960	226	178	129	80	46	13	0	0	0	0	0
1,960	2,000	232	184	135	86	50	17	0	0	0	0	0

MARRIED Persons—MONTHLY Payroll Period

(For Wages Paid through December 2013)

And the wages are—		And the number of withholding allowances claimed is —										
At least	But less than	0	1	2	3	4	5	6	7	8	9	10
		The amount of income tax to be withheld is—										
$ 0	$ 680	$ 0	$ 0	$ 0	$ 0	$ 0	$ 0	$ 0	$ 0	$0	$0	$0
680	720	1	0	0	0	0	0	0	0	0	0	0
720	760	5	0	0	0	0	0	0	0	0	0	0
760	800	9	0	0	0	0	0	0	0	0	0	0
800	840	13	0	0	0	0	0	0	0	0	0	0
840	880	17	0	0	0	0	0	0				
880	920	21	0	0	0	0	0	0				
920	960	25	0	0	0	0	0	0				
960	1,000	29	0	0	0	0	0	0				
1,000	1,040	33	0	0	0	0	0	0				
1,040	1,080	37	4	0	0	0	0	0				
1,080	1,120	41	8	0	0	0	0	0				
1,120	1,160	45	12	0	0	0	0	0	0	0	0	0
1,160	1,200	49	16	0	0	0	0	0	0	0	0	0
1,200	1,240	53	20	0	0	0	0	0	0	0	0	0
1,240	1,280	57	24	0	0	0	0	0	0	0	0	0
1,280	1,320	61	28	0	0	0	0	0	0	0	0	0
1,320	1,360	65	32	0	0	0	0	0	0	0	0	0
1,360	1,400	69	36	4	0	0	0	0	0	0	0	0
1,400	1,440	73	40	8	0	0	0	0	0	0	0	0
1,440	1,480	77	44	12	0	0	0	0	0	0	0	0
1,480	1,520	81	48	16	0	0	0	0	0	0	0	0
1,520	1,560	85	52	20	0	0	0	0	0	0	0	0
1,560	1,600	89	56	24	0	0	0	0	0	0	0	0
1,600	1,640	93	60	28	0	0	0	0	0	0	0	0
1,640	1,680	97	64	32	0	0	0	0	0	0	0	0
1,680	1,720	101	68	36	3	0	0	0	0	0	0	0
1,720	1,760	105	72	40	7	0	0	0	0	0	0	0
1,760	1,800	109	76	44	11	0	0	0	0	0	0	0

MONTHLY MARRIED PERSONS

➤ Compare your paycheck details for Mary and Max as shown below:

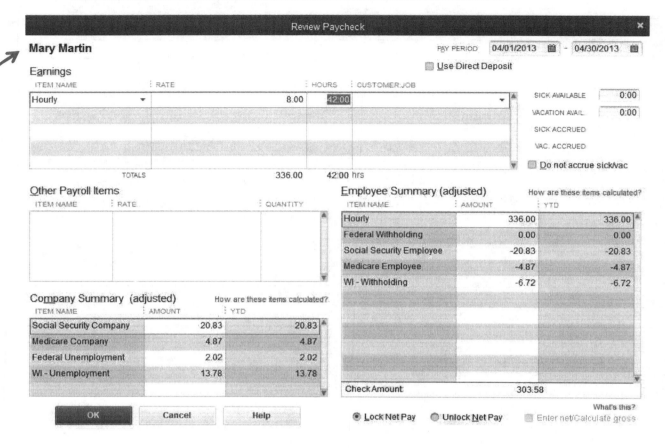

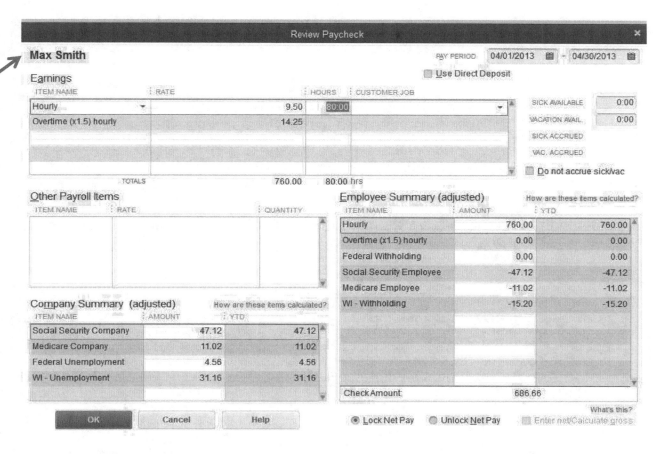

> Print/PDF paycheck stubs to submit at month-end.

> Create an Excel worksheet to track year-to-date gross wages for Mary and Max for FUTA and SUTA wage limits

Gross Pay for Wage Limits: FUTA & SUTA			
	Mary	Max	
30-Apr	336	760	

4/30   Month-end tasks:

> Dave reviews Unpaid Bills Detail report and approves payment for invoices due, check # 1019. Watch discount period.

> Prepare first quarter Wisconsin sales tax return. Print first quarter Sales Tax Liability report (under Vendors and Payables or Manage Sales Tax icon).

D & M Yard Services
Sales Tax Liability
January through March 2013

	Total Sales	Non-Taxable Sales	Taxable Sales	Tax Rate	Tax Collected	Sales Tax Payable As of Mar 31, 13
▾ WI Dept of Revenue						
Wisconsin sales tax ▸	2,242.00 ◂	1,480.00	762.00	5.0%	38.10	38.10
Total WI Dept of Revenue	2,242.00	1,480.00	762.00		38.10	38.10
TOTAL	2,242.00	1,480.00	762.00		38.10	38.10

Reconcile to taxable sales per the general ledger for the quarter: calculate total sales for *quarter* less tax exempt sales (to Forest Hill School) to equal taxable sales.

D & M Yard Services
General Ledger
As of March 31, 2013

Type	Date	Num	Adj	Name	Memo	Split	Debit	Credit	Balance
Total Opening Balance Equity									0.00
Fertilizing Income									**0.00**
Total Fertilizing Income									0.00
Installation Services									**0.00**
Total Installation Services									0.00
Landscaping Services									**0.00**
Invoice	03/12/2013	1		Davidson Foods	Deliver and ...	Accounts Re...		210.00	-210.00
Invoice	03/22/2013	2		Forest Hill School	Spread and ...	Accounts Re...		560.00	-770.00
Total Landscaping Services							0.00	770.00	-770.00
Lawn Cutting & Trimming									**0.00**
Total Lawn Cutting & Trimming									0.00
Maintenance Services									**0.00**
Total Maintenance Services									0.00
Mulch Sales									**0.00**
Invoice	03/12/2013	1		Davidson Foods	Mulch	Accounts Re...		552.00	-552.00
Invoice	03/22/2013	2		Forest Hill School	Mulch	Accounts Re...		920.00	-1,472.00
Total Mulch Sales							0.00	1,472.00	-1,472.00

Reconciliation:

Landscaping Services: $ 770 per general ledger

Mulch Sales   1472 per general ledger

   TOTAL SALES $2242 for first quarter

Less: Non-taxable   1480 to Forest Hill School

1st Qtr. Taxable Sales $ 762 YES, agrees with taxable sales per Sales Tax
Liability report above.

Print and complete Wisconsin Sales and Use Tax Return, ST-12 (source: WI Dept. of Revenue website). Pay amount due, check #1020; note discount given on line 19 represents a small remuneration for collecting and remitting the sales tax and should be credited to a miscellaneous income account.

> Preview monthly statements for all customers and compare to Customer Balance Summary or Detail report.

D & M Yard Services
Customer Balance Summary
All Transactions

	◇ Apr 30, 13 ◇
Forest Hill School	▶ 282.00 ◀
Jacksonville Industrial Park	369.60
Joe Calhoun	165.90
Larry Laxson	129.15
Nottingham Condominium Complex	731.85
Paul Garrett	165.90
Walter Brown	444.15
TOTAL	2,288.55

> Prepare monthly draw of $1000, check #1021.

> Reconcile cash account for April and compare your trial balance to the following; review and make corrections if needed. NOTE: The bank reconciliations and trial balances were included through this first month with payroll. Future reports will not be posted in each month; your instructor will post reports for your review.

D & M Yard Services
Reconciliation Detail
All Transactions

Type	Date	Num	Name	Clr	Amount	Balance
Check	04/01/2013	1011	John Smith	✔	-750.00	-2,487.45
Check	04/07/2013	1012	American Insurance	✔	-1,410.00	-3,897.45
Check	04/15/2013	1015	IRS	✔	-500.00	-4,397.45
Check	04/15/2013	1014	Credit Card Servic...	✔	-342.80	-4,740.25
Check	04/15/2013	1016	WI Dept of Revenue	✔	-150.00	-4,890.25
Bill Pmt -Check	04/15/2013	1013	JS Garden Supply	✔	-126.91	-5,017.16
Check	04/30/2013			✔	-15.00	-5,032.16
		Total Checks and Payments			-5,032.16	-5,032.16

	Deposits and Credits - 1 item					
Deposit	04/03/2013			✔	2,234.50	2,234.50
		Total Deposits and Credits			2,234.50	2,234.50

	Total Cleared Transactions				-2,797.66	-2,797.66

Cleared Balance					-2,797.66	15,709.90

	Uncleared Transactions					
	Checks and Payments - 5 items					
Check	04/30/2013	1021	Dave Michaels		-1,000.00	-1,000.00
Paycheck	04/30/2013	1018	Max Smith		-686.66	-1,686.66
Paycheck	04/30/2013	1017	Mary Martin		-303.58	-1,990.24
Bill Pmt -Check	04/30/2013	1019	JS Garden Supply		-149.50	-2,139.74
Sales Tax Paym...	04/30/2013	1020	WI Dept of Revenue		-28.10	-2,167.84
		Total Checks and Payments			-2,167.84	-2,167.84

	Total Uncleared Transactions				-2,167.84	-2,167.84

Register Balance as of 04/30/2013					-4,965.50	13,542.06

Ending Balance					-4,965.50	13,542.06

> Review the April trial balance below, particularly noting new payroll accounts:

D & M Yard Services
Trial Balance
As of April 30, 2013

	Apr 30, 13	
	Debit	Credit
D&M Yard Services Checking Acct	13,542.06	
Petty Cash	200.00	
Accounts Receivable	2,288.55	
Inventory Asset	5,030.94	
Prepaid Insurance	1,175.00	
Undeposited Funds	0.00	
Lawn and Landscaping Equipment	4,500.00	
Office Equipment	787.50	
Truck	18,200.00	
Leasehold Improvements	850.00	
Security Deposit	1,000.00	
Accounts Payable		4,700.00
Credit Card Payable		66.87
FICA Payable		167.68
FIT Withholding	0.00	
FUTA Payable		6.58
Payroll Liabilities	0.00	
Sales Tax Payable		95.55
SUTA Payable		44.94
SWT Payable		21.92
D. Michaels, Capital		48,200.00
D. Michaels, Drawing	3,340.81	
Fertilizing Income		324.00
Landscaping Services		1,295.00
Lawn Cutting & Trimming		980.00
Mulch Sales		1,702.00
Sales Discounts	45.60	
Seeding Income		134.00
Fertilizing Costs	269.10	
Mulch Costs	1,424.50	
Purchase Discounts		133.79
Seeding Costs	114.26	
Auto and Truck Expenses	195.00	
Bank Service Charges	60.00	
FICA Tax Expense	83.84	
Field Wages	1,096.00	
FUTA Tax Expense	6.58	
Insurance Expense	235.00	
Office Supplies	709.47	
Office Wages	0.00	
Payroll Expenses	0.00	
Rent Expense	1,500.00	
Small Tools and Equipment	923.18	
SUTA Tax Expense	44.94	
Telephone Expense	110.00	
Utilities	150.00	
Miscellaneous Income		10.00
TOTAL	57,882.33	57,882.33

Credit Card Services, Inc.

D & M Yard Services

Statement Date: 4/5/2013

Amount Due: 342.80

Due Date: 4/15/2013

Charge Summary:

3/5	Gas To Go	52.00
3/12	Deli Stop	12.80
3/17	Cell World	60.00
3/20	Gas To Go	68.00
3/26	Utility Service Corp.	150.00

XYZ Bank

D & M Yard Services

Acct. # 745-1332   4/1/2013 thru 4/30/2013

Beg. Balance: 18507.56

Deposits & CM

4/3   2234.50

Checks & DM

#1003	387.45
#1009	850.00
#1010	500.00
#1011	750.00
#1012	1410.00
#1013	126.91
#1014	342.80
#1015	500.00
#1016	150.00
4/30 SC	15.00

Ending Balance: $ 15709.90

Receipt: 4/3/2013

ABC Food Store   7.86

This receipt is to support the petty cash disbursement; should be filed with your petty cash sheet.

April Questions

1. Explain the difference between customer invoices and statements.

2. Review financial statements, Profit & Loss Standard and Balance Sheet Standard. List 3 items to edit at year-end when the financial statements are exported into Excel. For example: placement of Sales Discounts.

3. Complete: a) Monthly Task List and b) your To Do/Follow-up Question List with at least two items to be addressed by your "manager"/teacher.

CHAPTER PRINT/SUBMISSION SUMMARY

Reminder: use option to submit reports as a PDF file.

1._____ Petty Cash Sheet, Excel or Word document (showing activity)

2. _____ 1040-ES and 1-ES

3. _____ Paycheck stubs and Excel file for wage limits

4._____ Sales Tax Liability Report & Sales Tax Return: ST-12

5._____ Bank Account Reconciliation

6. _____Trial Balance

7._____ Profit & Loss Standard for Question #2

8._____ Balance Sheet Standard for Question #2

9._____ Questions #1 & 2 (list of 3 items)

10. _____Task List/To Do/Question List

APRIL TASK LIST

Check here if completed	Task	Initials
	Review of Unpaid Bills Detail Report	
	Preview monthly statements for all customers and compare to Customer Detail report	
	Create Excel file for year-to-date payroll amounts	
	Review of Profit and Loss and Balance Sheet	
	Verify cash balance on trial balance equals cash balance on bank reconciliation	
	Review trial balance for completeness and accuracy	
	Back up your monthly transactions to an external destination (e.g. flash drive), changing file name to the month	

To Do/Follow-up/Question List

May Transactions/Activities

NOTE: As we continue, transactions will not include detail instructions on how to record the transaction; you are to refer to prior months' transactions or use QuickBooks Help.

Monthly information/tasks; to be completed from MAY THROUGH DECEMBER!

1. Each time you start QuickBooks the prompt to Enter Memorized Transactions will come up; we will only select the one month's insurance adjustment.
2. Pay rent on 1st of each month, using the memorized transaction set up in April.
3. Review and record credit card statement on the 5th of each month, payable on the 15th.
4. Dave reviews A/P Aging Detail and approves invoices due for payment on the 15th of each month.
5. As of May 1 contracted customers and their lawn maintenance times are:
   Brown: 2 hours
   Calhoun: 3 hours
   Forest Hill School: 4 hours
   Jacksonville Ind. Park: 6 hours
   Laxson: 2 hours
   Garrett: 3 hours
   Nottingham Condos: 8 hours

   AT MONTH-END:
6. Prepare/calculate monthly payroll.
7. Update Excel worksheet for each payroll.
8. Dave reviews A/P Aging Detail or Unpaid Bills Detail and approves invoices due for payment on the 30th/31st of each month. Note: sales tax will be reported and paid each **quarter**, due at the end of the month following the quarter.
9. Review Customer Balance Detail; preview monthly statements. We will only print customer statements each quarter in this project.
10. Prepare monthly draw of $1000, unless otherwise noted.
11. Reconcile cash account.
12. Review trial balance, verifying that the cash balance per ledger equals reconciled balance.

5/2   Returned 2 boxwood bushes to JS Supply for credit on account, credit memo #501. (If necessary, use QuickBooks Help) Follow policy on *vendor* credit memos per the company information, Dave will initial A/P Aging Detail 5/15 report for credit memo.

5/2 Changed Mary, office manager, to salaried at $1280 per month for the busy season of May – September.

5/3 Hired student, Brian Jones, address: 300 Main St., Landscape, WI 53022, SS#: 673-22-8585, <u>exempt</u> from federal and state withholding, as part-time summer help at $7.25 an hour. (If necessary, review adding employees from March transactions.)

5/7 New section of Jacksonville Industrial Park opened. Spread 4 yards of topsoil, 2 bags of seed, 4 bales of straw, and 15 yards of mulch. Planted 4 boxwood bushes, 4 of the 36" arbor vitae and 2 of the 5' arbor vitae, and 16 hours of landscaping labor. Invoice for work performed.

5/7 Received payment in full from April's customer statements with the exception of Walter Brown's invoice for mulch job on April 2, still outstanding. (Use 4/30/2013 Customer Balance Detail report to help determine receipts and calculate discounts!) REMINDER: discounts: residential n/10 from statement date and commercial 2/10, n/30 (<u>from statement</u> date). Record deposit.

5/11 Completed spring clean-up <u>AND</u> regular lawn maintenance for ALL contracted customers; ***additional*** <u>time</u> incurred listed below. (Use memorized transactions.) Record all income to Lawn Cutting & Trimming. Create invoices.

Brown: 1 hour

Calhoun: 1 hour

Forest Hill School: no additional time incurred

Jacksonville Industrial Park: 3 hours

Laxson: 1 hour

Garrett: 2 hours

Nottingham Condominiums: 3 hours

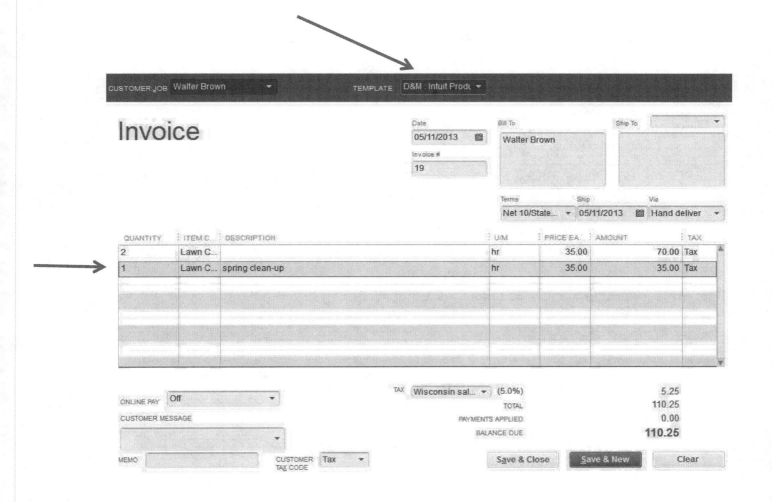

5/12   Received complaint from Walter Brown about April's mulch work; credited his account for one hour of landscaping labor, credit memo #201. Follow policy on credit memos as outlined in company information. Apply to the April mulch invoice.

5/18   Completed lawn maintenance for ALL contracted customers; create invoices.

5/25   Due to spring growing season, completed lawn maintenance for ALL contracted customers; noting Jacksonville Industrial Park will now require 3 additional hours each time, starting with <u>this</u> invoice, replace memorized transaction for Jacksonville. Create invoices.

5/27   Purchased string and oil for trimmer for $37.80 on credit card. Record.

5/31   Prepare payroll:

Mary - salaried (ck. #1025)   Max: 162 hours (2 OT) (ck. #1026)

Brian: 28 hours (ck. #1024)

Note: Mary will have federal withholding this pay period; use payroll withholding tables found in last month's activities/transactions.

<u>Update</u> the Excel payroll worksheet started with the April payroll.

5/31   Perform month-end tasks. (See list above.)

Credit Card Services, Inc.

D & M Yard Services

Statement Date: 5/5/2013

Amount Due: 422.87

Due Date: 5/15/2013

Charge Summary:

Date	Description	Amount
4/2	TV & Appliance	30.45
4/5	Office City	36.42
4/12	Gas To Go	78.00
4/17	Cell World	60.00
4/20	Gas To Go	68.00
4/26	Utility Service Corp.	150.00

XYZ Bank

D & M Yard Services

Acct. # 745-1332

5/1/2013 thru 5/31/2013

Beg. Balance   15709.90

Deposits & CM

5/7   1945.88

Checks & DM

#1017	303.58	1021	1000.00
#1018	686.66	1022	750.00
#1019	149.50	1023	422.87
#1020	28.10		
5/31 SC	15.00		

Ending Balance: $ 14300.07

Print the task list below on a separate sheet of brightly colored paper (if possible) to use as carry forward schedule; meaning to be brought forward as a reminder to complete these tasks each month!

Monthly information/tasks; to be completed from MAY THROUGH DECEMBER!

1. Each time you start QuickBooks the prompt to Enter Memorized Transactions will come up; we will only select the one month's insurance adjustment.
2. Pay rent on 1st of each month, using the memorized transaction set up in April.
3. Review and record credit card statement on the 5th of each month, payable on the 15th.
4. Dave reviews A/P Aging Detail and approves invoices due for payment on the 15th of each month.
5. **As of May 1** contracted customers and their lawn maintenance times are:
   Brown: 2 hours
   Calhoun: 3 hours
   Forest Hill School: 4 hours
   Jacksonville Ind. Park: 6 hours
   Laxson: 2 hours
   Garrett: 3 hours
   Nottingham Condos: 8 hours

   ## AT MONTH-END:

6. Prepare/calculate monthly payroll.
7. Update Excel worksheet for each payroll.
8. Dave reviews A/P Aging Detail or Unpaid Bills Detail and approves invoices due for payment on the 30th/31st of each month. Note: sales tax will be reported and paid each **quarter**, due at the end of the month following the quarter.
9. Review Customer Balance Detail; preview monthly statements; we will only print customer statements each quarter in this project.
10. Prepare monthly draw of $1000, unless otherwise noted.
11. Reconcile cash account.
    Review trial balance, verifying that the cash balance per ledger equals reconciled balance.

May Questions

1. Print/PDF Journal report for 1/1/2013 through 5/31/2013; review entries for transactions entered year-to-date.

2. Complete: a) Monthly Task List and b) your To Do/Follow-up Question List with at least two items to be addressed by your "manager"/teacher.

CHAPTER PRINT/SUBMISSION SUMMARY

1.____ Customer Balance Detail with credit memo approval (export to Excel to note approval)

2.____ Bank Reconciliation

3.____ Trial Balance

4.____ Question #1 – Journal report 1/1/2013 through 5/31/2013

5.____ Task List/To Do/Question List

MAY TASK LIST

Check here if completed	Task	Initials
	Review of Unpaid Bills Detail Report	
	Credit memo prepared and approved	
	Preview customer statements	
	Verify cash balance on trial balance equals cash balance on bank reconciliation	
	Review trial balance for completeness and accuracy	
	Back up your monthly transactions to an external destination (e.g. flash drive), changing file name to the month	
	REMINDER: Complete month-end tasks	

To Do/Follow-up/Question List

June Transactions/Activities

Reminder of monthly tasks!

6/1   Dave and Sue inherited $10,000 from Sue's uncle; this total amount was invested into the business.

6/1   Completed lawn maintenance for ALL contracted customers; create invoices.

6/4   Spread 1 yard of topsoil and a bag of seed. Planted 2 boxwood bushes at Davidson Foods, 3 hours; prepare/email invoice.

6/7   Completed some general clean-up at Forest Hill School, 20 hours.

6/8   Completed lawn maintenance for ALL contracted customers; prepare invoices.

6/10   Received full payment from all May statements <u>except</u> for Brown's April invoice; also No payment was received from Jacksonville Industrial Park. (Reminder: Use Customer Balance Detail report as of 5/31 to help determine receipts and calculate discounts!)

6/12   Paid PP Equipment $309.50 for oil change on tractor; issued check #1029.

6/15   Completed lawn maintenance for ALL contracted customers; prepare invoices.

6/15   Make federal and Wisconsin estimated tax payments, checks #1031 and 1032. Complete 1040-ES and WI 1-ES for 2nd quarter.

6/16   Received full payment from Jacksonville Industrial Park for May statement.

6/17   Purchased snacks and drinks for office with petty cash, $32.45.

6/22   Completed lawn maintenance for ALL contracted customers; prepare invoices.

6/25   Spread 10 yards of topsoil in the Jacksonville Industrial Park, 5 hours.

6/30   Prepare payroll.

Mary - salaried (ck. #1034)   Max: 164 hours (ck. #1035)

Brian: 65 hours (ck. #1033)

6/30   Perform month-end tasks.

Reminder: since it is end of quarter, print/PDF customer statements.

Credit Card Services, Inc.

D & M Yard Services

Statement Date: 6/5/2013

Amount Due: 581.70

Due Date: 6/15/2013

Charge Summary:

5/2	ABC Food Store	124.72
5/4	Max's Drug Store	15.18
5/7	Gas To Go	120.00
5/17	Cell World	60.00
5/18	Gas To Go	74.00
5/26	Utility Service Corp.	150.00
5/27	PP Equipment	37.80

XYZ Bank

D & M Yard Services

Acct. # 745-1332   6/1/2013 thru 6/30/2013

Beg. Balance: $14300.07

Deposits & CM

6/1	10000.00
6/10	2670.25
6/16	2674.98

Checks & DM

1024	187.47	1029	309.50
1025	1074.48	1030	581.70
1026	1399.07	1031	500.00
1027	1000.00	1032	150.00
1028	750.00		
6/30 SC	15.00		

Ending Balance: $ 23678.08

Receipt   6/17/2013

ABC Food Store

Snacks   32.45

June Questions

1. Determine if the inheritance received by Dave and Sue is taxable income on their personal income tax return; copy and paste the answer in a Word document as found in an IRS publication.

2. As completed in March, see task list for quarterly comparison of control account balances to subsidiary ledger balances. Document in your Word document started above.

3. As a measure of internal control over sequentially numbered invoices, prepare report of numerically sorted invoices for quarter from the Customer Center/Transactions/Invoice.

4. Complete: a) Monthly Task List and b) your To Do/Follow-up Question List with at least two items to be addressed by your "manager"/teacher.

5. Prepare a short 3 minute oral presentation addressing 2 managerial/business-related (e.g. internal controls, marketing...) and 3 financial-related items. Submit a presentation outline. Note: instructor will select students each quarter.

CHAPTER PRINT/SUBMISSION SUMMARY

1._____ 1040-ES & WI 1-ES

2._____ Customer statements

3._____ Subsidiary ledger reports for A/R, A/P and Inventory used in question #2

4._____ Report of numerically sorted invoices for quarter

5._____ Check Register for April – June with Dave's initials to indicate reviewed

6._____ Bank Account Reconciliation

7._____ Trial Balance

8. _____ Questions # 1 & 2

9._____ Task List/To Do/Question List

10._____ Presentation outline for selected students

JUNE TASK LIST

Check here if completed	Task	Initials
	Review of Unpaid Bills Detail Reports	
	Compare A/R control account balance (A/R on trial balance) to a detail report of the A/R subsidiary ledger	
	Compare A/P control account balance (A/P on trial balance) to a detail report of the A/P subsidiary ledger	
	Compare Inventory control account balance (Inventory on trial balance) to a detail report of the Inventory subsidiary ledger	
	Prepare report of numerically sorted invoices from the Customer Center/Transactions/Invoice	
	Review check detail for April - June, Dave indicates review with his initials on report (see cash-related information at beginning of project) Export report into Excel to note initials.	
	Review general ledger for April – June (NOTE: on screen ONLY; no printing)	
	Verify cash balance on trial balance equals cash balance on bank reconciliation	
	Review trial balance for completeness and accuracy	
	Back up your monthly transactions to an external destination (e.g. flash drive), changing file name to the month	

To Do/Follow-up/Question List

July Transactions/Activities

Reminder of monthly tasks!

7/1   Offer health insurance and traditional 401k to Mary and Max. The health insurance is a 50/50 plan (not a cafeteria or flexible spending plan); 50% employer paid, 50% employee paid; the married plan is $400 per month in **TOTAL**; the single plan $180 per month in **TOTAL**. For the 401k, Mary and Max will contribute 2% of their gross monthly pay and D & M will match these contributions. Both Mary and Max will take advantage of both of these benefits. Update payroll settings & the individual employee's payroll information for these benefits. Vendor information: Healthcare Insurance (account #: 12345) and Investors, Inc. (account #: 67890); and NO regular payment schedule. Health insurance will be a flat amount; 401k a percentage.

NOTE: Not ALL screens shown!

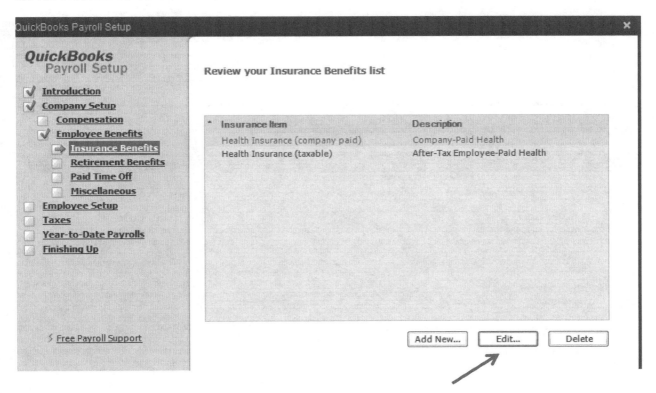

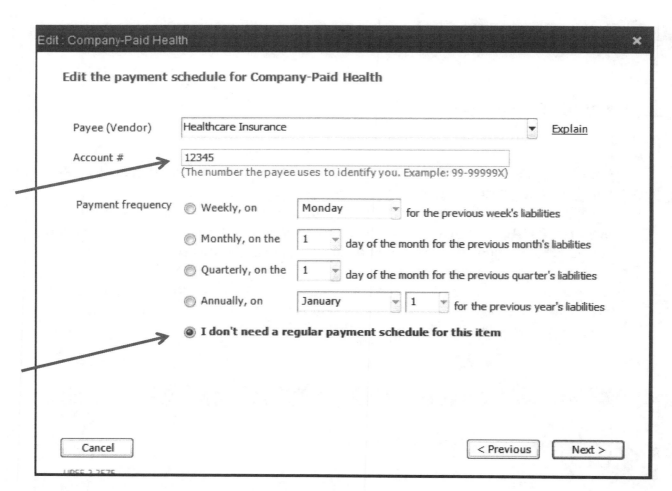

Accept accounts here, we will edit the payroll items:

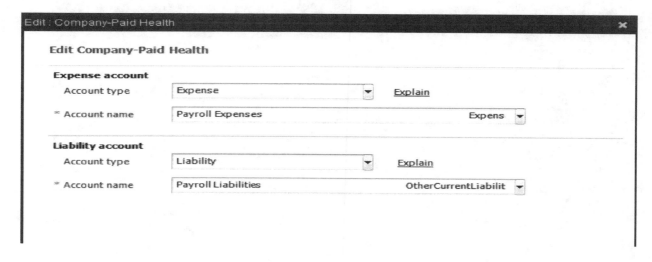

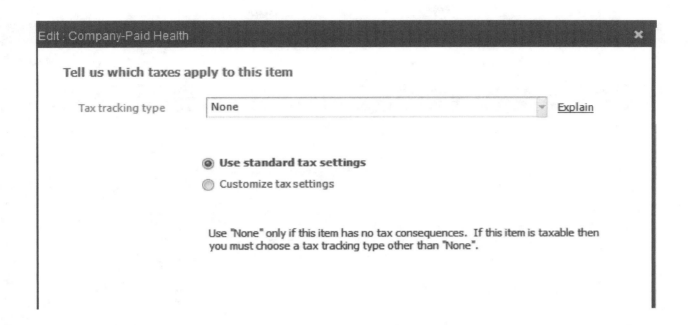

NOTE: Can only enter one amount here, use single plan amount; you will have to edit Max's paycheck detail for the married plan amount.

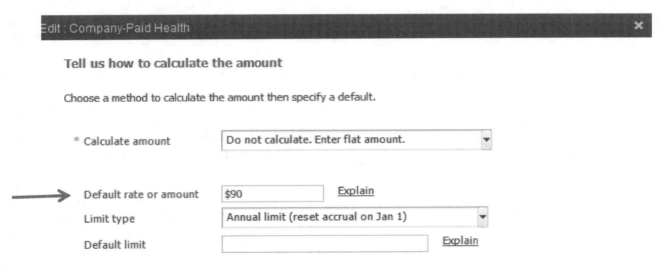

Next, Employee List:

Turn on 401k and Health Insurance:

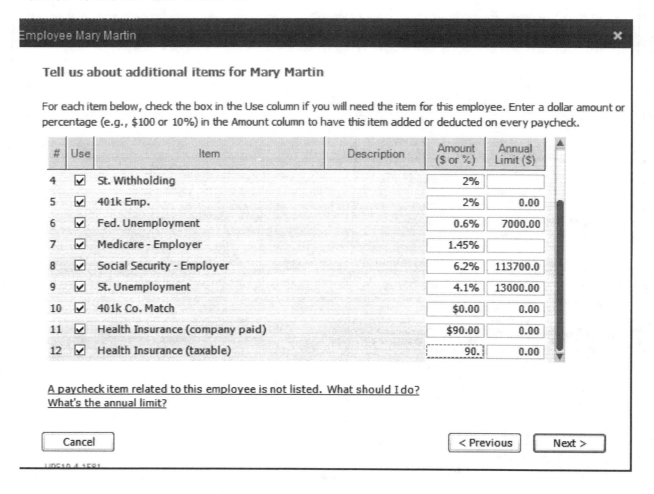

Review/Edit Mary and Max's employee payroll information on their individual employee information screens.

Add accounts for 401k Payable, 401k Employer Contribution, Health Insurance Payable and Health Insurance – Employer. Edit 401k and health insurance items for these new accounts.

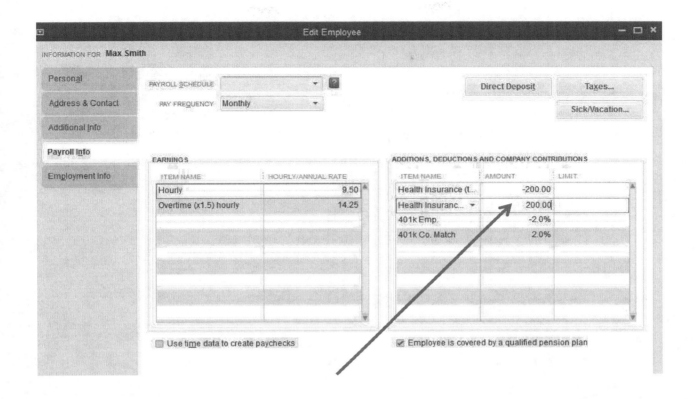

7/3   Spread 10 yards of topsoil and 3 bags of seed at Forest Hill School; 12 hours; create invoice.

7/10   Received full payment from all customers from June statements except for Brown's April invoice.

7/13   Paid $1000 on balance owed to PP Equipment for equipment previously purchased; issued check. (Note: unpaid balance will start accruing interest on 7/15 at a 9% annual rate, interest will be paid when next payment is made, all future payments will be *specifically* identified in the monthly transactions.)

7/13   Completed lawn maintenance for ALL contracted customers; create invoices.

7/14   Purchased printer paper, envelopes, ink and other miscellaneous office supplies, charged $65.63 to credit card.

7/15 Review Unpaid Bills Detail; pay any amounts due. Prepare WT-6, Wisconsin state withholding report from the Wisconsin Department of Revenue website (see example below), and pay the amount due for 2nd quarter WI withholding. Mary Martin, our office manager, will file these reports. Use Pay Liabilities.

FORM WT-6
WITHHOLDING TAX DEPOSIT REPORT
WISCONSIN DEPARTMENT OF REVENUE
PO Box 930931
Milwaukee WI 53293-0931

W-006 (R. 12-12)
DO NOT FOLD, BEND, STAPLE, OR TEAR

Choose FILING FREQUENCY with drop down arrow below.

FILING FREQUENCY

NAME

ADDRESS

CITY   STATE ZIP

I certify that this report is correct.   Signature:

Title:

The scan line must contain your Tax Account Number in order to be processed. Please do not use the PRINT button until you have tabbed out of the period covered field.

TAX ACCOUNT NUMBER   CALENDAR YEAR

FEIN

Choose PERIOD COVERED BY THIS REPORT with drop down arrow below.

PERIOD COVERED BY THIS REPORT

WISCONSIN TAX WITHHELD
$.

Date:

Tele:

— DO NOT WRITE IN SPACE BELOW —

931 999999999999999995 999995

Use the Reports Tab on the check and review the Transaction Journal.

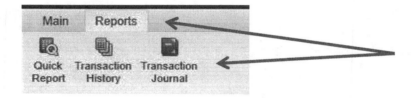

7/17 Planted 4 36" arbor vitae, 2 5' arbor vitae; laid 20 yards of topsoil and 25 yards of mulch at the Nottingham Condominium Complex, 30 hours; create invoice.

7/25 Bought oil and miscellaneous equipment supplies from PP Equipment, $43.05 charged to credit card.

7/31 Perform all month-end tasks including:

Payroll Reminder: 401k employee/employer and health insurance employee/employer start in July. NOTE: federal **AND** state withholding are calculated AFTER the 401k deduction; **YOU** will have to RE-CALCULATE state withholding! 401k contributions and health insurance premiums will be paid quarterly.

Mary: (#1041)   Max: 167 hours (#1042)   Brian: 42 hours (#1043)

Reminder of draw each month!

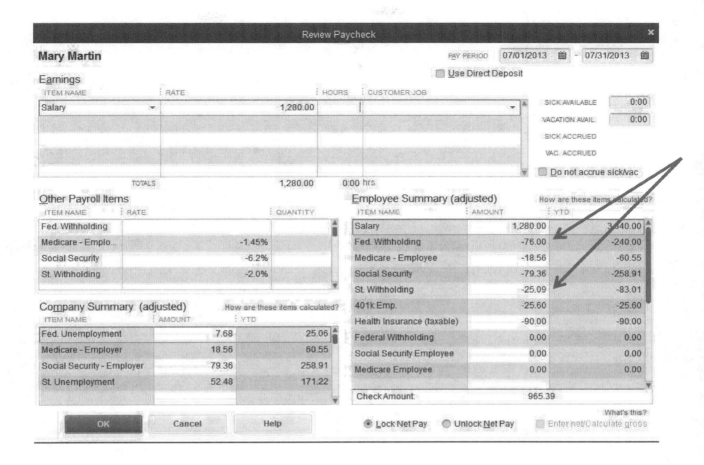

> Print 2nd quarter Sales Tax Liability report, complete return (WI ST-12) and pay 2nd quarter sales tax. (#1045).

> Complete 2nd quarter 941 and UCT-101 (WI unemployment) and pay amounts due for 2nd quarter (#1046 and 1047 respectively).

> 941: Go to Employees/Payroll Tax Forms & W-2s/Tax Form Worksheets in Excel/for this quarter/ 4/1/2013 – 6/30/2013. Compare amounts on worksheet to 2nd quarter payroll summary report. To enter Federal Withholding Tax: right click on cell, clear contents and enter the federal withholding amount for this quarter. Use amounts on this worksheet to complete a Form 941 from the IRS website. Note that Total deposits for the quarter should equal the balance in the FICA Payable and FIT Withholding accounts per your 6/30/2013 trial balance. See screen shot below, noting fraction of cents adjustment line:

Read the separate instructions before you complete Form 941. Type or print within the boxes.

1	Number of employees who received wages, tips, or other compensation for the pay period including: Mar. 12 (Quarter 1), June 12 (Quarter 2), Sept. 12 (Quarter 3), or Dec. 12 (Quarter 4)	1	3
2	Wages, tips, and other compensation	2	7455 . 75
3	Federal income tax withheld from wages, tips, and other compensation	3	164 .
4	If no wages, tips, and other compensation are subject to social security or Medicare tax	☐ Check and go to line 6.	

	Column 1		Column 2
5a Taxable social security wages . .	7455 . 75	× .124 =	924 . 51
5b Taxable social security tips . . .	.	× .124 =	.
5c Taxable Medicare wages & tips . .	7455 . 75	× .029 =	216 . 22
5d Taxable wages & tips subject to Additional Medicare Tax withholding	.	× .009 =	.

5e	Add Column 2 from lines 5a, 5b, 5c, and 5d	5e	1304 . 73
5f	Section 3121(q) Notice and Demand—Tax due on unreported tips (see instructions) . .	5f	.
6	Total taxes before adjustments. Add lines 3, 5e, and 5f	6	.
7	Current quarter's adjustment for fractions of cents	7	. 01
8	Current quarter's adjustment for sick pay	8	.
9	Current quarter's adjustments for tips and group-term life insurance	9	.
10	Total taxes after adjustments. Combine lines 6 through 9	10	1304 . 72
11	Total deposits for this quarter, including overpayment applied from a prior quarter and overpayments applied from Form 941-X, 941-X (PR), 944-X, 944-X (PR), or 944-X (SP) filed in the current quarter	11	1304 . 72
12	Balance due. If line 10 is more than line 11, enter the difference and see instructions . . .	12	0 .

➢ Go to Pay Liabilities and make 2nd quarter deposit (check #1046). Review transaction journal for correct journal entry.

- State Unemployment: Wisconsin Form UC-101. Create Excel worksheet/State SUI Wage Listing (this is the second page for the UC-101). Prepare UC-101 found on the Dept. of Workforce Development website.

			1st Month	Number of Employees	2nd Month	Number of Employees	3rd Month	Number of Employees
1. U.I. ACCOUNT NUMBER 876543-211-1	**2. QUARTER** 2	**YEAR** 13				2		3		3

1b. INTERNET ACCESS NUMBER
http://dwd.wisconsin.gov/uitax

Item		Amount
9. TOTAL COVERED WAGE Must agree with total wages on Wage Report	7,455	75
10. LESS EXCLUSIONS FOR WAGES OVER $14,000 (See instructions on back of form.)		
11. DEFINED (TAXABLE) PAYROLL Item 9 minus Item 10 THIS LINE MUST BE COMPLETED	7,455	75
12. TAX RATE:	.0410	
13. TAX DUE: Multiply Item 11 by Item 12	305	69
14. INTEREST DUE: If filed after due date, compute interest on Item 13 above. (See instructions on back of form.)		
15. LATE FILING FEE: If Wage Report (UC-7823) is filed after due date, add fee. (See instructions on back of form.)		
16. LESS ELECTRONIC FUND TRANSFER PAYMENT		
17. LESS CREDIT AVAILABLE as of		
18. TOTAL AMOUNT ENCLOSED WITH THIS REPORT	305	69

3. REPORT AND PAYMENT DUE   4. ACCOUNT NUMBER

5. FEIN
39-121 2121

6. EMPLOYER TELEPHONE NO./EMAIL

7. EMPLOYER NAME AND ADDRESS

D & M Yard Services

900 Main St.

Landscape, WI 53022

19. I CERTIFY THE TAX AND WAGE REPORTS ARE CORRECT.

RETURN THIS FORM AND ANY PAYMENT DUE. MAKE CHECK OR MONEY ORDER PAYABLE TO: DIVISION OF UNEMPLOYMENT INSURANCE. FOR INFORMATION CALL (608) 261-6700.

- Go to Pay Liabilities and make 2nd quarter payment (check #1047). Review transaction journal on check for correct journal entry.

- Pay 940 deposit if required, refer to instructions for IRS Form 940 to determine when 940 deposits are due.

Credit Card Services, Inc.

D & M Yard Services

Statement Date: 7/5/2013

Amount Due: 477.00

Due Date: 7/15/2013

Charge Summary:

6/2	Gas To Go	82.00
6/15	Gas To Go	130.00
6/17	Cell World	60.00
6/25	Gas To Go	55.00
6/26	Utility Service Corp.	150.00

XYZ Bank

D & M Yard Services

Acct. # 745-1332

7/1/2013 thru 7/31/2013

Beg. Balance: $ 23678.08

Deposits & CM

7/10   5787.56

Checks & DM

1033	435.20	1039	477.00
1034	1074.48	1040	135.63
1035	1424.82		
1036	1000.00		
1037	750.00		
1038	1000.00		

7/31   SC   15.00

Ending Balance: $ 23153.51

July Questions

1. Reconcile Sales Tax Revenue Summary Report (Manage Sales Tax) to sales accounts in the general ledger for 2nd quarter. Calculate total sales for *quarter* less tax exempt sales (to Forest Hill School) to equal taxable sales. Show reconciliation on sales tax revenue report.

2. Compare amounts on the 2nd quarter Payroll Summary report to amounts on Excel worksheets used to complete 941 and UCT-101 and respective general ledger accounts. Show comparison on Payroll Summary Report exported into Excel. See example:

941 TAXES	
FIT	164
SS -ee	108.1
Med -ee	462.26
SS-er	108.1
Med -er	462.26
TIES TO 941	1304.72

Per June 30th trial balance: FICA Payable   1140.72

FIT Withholding   164.00

TOTAL   1304.72

3. Print (copy and paste or screen shot in Word document) the 940 deposit requirements per IRS. (only deposit requirements)

4. Complete: a) Monthly Task List and b) your To Do/Follow-up Question List with at least two items to be addressed by your "manager"/teacher.

CHAPTER PRINT/SUBMISSION SUMMARY

1._____ WT-6

2._____ Bank Account Reconciliation

3._____ Trial Balance

4._____ Question #1 – Sales Tax Liability Report and ST-12

5._____ Question #2 – Payroll Summary Report with comparison, Excel files for 941 and UCT-101, Forms 941 and UCT-101

6._____ Question #3 – Support

7._____ Task List/To Do/Question List

JULY TASK LIST

Check here if completed	Task	Initials
	Review of Unpaid Bills Detail Report	
	Preview customer statements	
	Print and review Payroll Summary report	
	Review Transaction Journal under reports on payment screen for WT-6 payment, 941 deposit and UCT-101 payment	
	Verify cash balance on trial balance equals cash balance on bank reconciliation	
	Review trial balance for completeness and accuracy	
	Back up your monthly transactions to an external destination (e.g. flash drive), changing file name to the month	

To Do/Follow-up/Question List

August Transactions/Activities

Reminder of monthly tasks!

8/6   Year-end close-out of bushes at JS Supply, picked up 6 boxwood bushes at $6.50 each and 4 5' arbor vitae at $12.50 each. Invoice 872, terms 2/10, n/30.

8/7   In preparation for the start of school at Forest Hill School, re-seeded areas laying 15 yards of topsoil, 2 bags of seed and 3 bags of straw, 5 yards of mulch, including general clean-up, 30 hours. Create invoice.

8/10   Received full payment from July statements except for Brown's April invoice, Forest Hill School, and Jacksonville Industrial Park.

8/10   Completed lawn maintenance for ALL contracted customers; create invoices.

8/13   Planted 5 boxwood bushes and 5 tall arbor vitae and spread 4 yards of topsoil and 10 yards of mulch, 20 hours, for Davidson Foods. Create invoice.

8/15   Review Unpaid Bills Detail; pay any amounts due, use outstanding credit memo on JS Supply invoice. Dave approved an additional $1000 payment to PP Equipment plus interest from July 15 through August 15 (should account for 31 days of interest using a 360 day year for calculation, interest = $28.68). *To account for the interest on this check, per QuickBooks Help Community:* **Split Vendor Payment between partial vendor bill and interest charge:** I am trying to make a partial payment on a vendor bill (in accounts payable already) that also includes interest. How do I split the payment between a partial payment on the vendor bill and interest expense?

ANSWER:

Enter a bill for the vendor for the interest. Pay a partial on the regular invoice and the interest.

8/22   Received payments from Davidson Foods for August work and from Forest Hill and Jacksonville Industrial Park for balances due from their July statements.

8/24   Completed lawn maintenance for ALL contracted customers; create invoices.

8/27   Ordered 20 bags of fertilizer at fall close-out price of $6/bag for fall applications from JS Supply. Prepare purchase order #2.

8/31   Had a company picnic for employees and families at Dave's house. Cost of $122.86 paid from petty cash.

8/31   Perform month-end tasks.

Payroll:

Mary - salaried (#1052)   Max: 150 hours due to seasonal/business needs (#1053)

Brian: 65 hours (# 1054) (last payroll for Brian as he is returning to school)

Credit Card Services, Inc.

D & M Yard Services

Statement Date: 8/5/2013

Amount Due: 612.85

Due Date: 8/15/2013

Charge Summary:

7/7	Gas To Go	85.00
7/14	Office City	65.63
7/17	Cell World	60.00
7/18	Gas To Go	125.00
7/25	PP Equipment	43.05
7/26	Utility Service Corp.	150.00
7/31	ABC Food Store	84.17

XYZ Bank

D & M Yard Services

Acct. # 745-1332

Beg. Balance: $23153.51

Deposits & CM

8/10	3487.22
8/22	2828.55

Checks & DM

1041	965.39	1047	305.69
1042	1231.69	1048	750.00
1043	281.20	1049	612.85
1044	1000.00	1050	61.32
1045	539.48	1051	1028.68
1046	1304.72		
8/31	SC 15.00		

Ending Balance: $21373.26

Receipt 8/30 for petty cash disbursement

ABC Food Store $ 122.86

August Questions

1. List 3 internal control procedures for petty cash.

2. Research and print (cut & paste in Word document) the income tax treatment of entertainment expenses as it pertains to the <u>company picnic</u>.

3. Complete: a) Monthly Task List (note tasks for completion) and b) your To Do/Follow-up Question List with at least two items to be addressed by your "manager"/teacher.

CHAPTER PRINT/SUBMISSION SUMMARY

1._____ Bank Account Reconciliation

2._____ Trial Balance

3._____ Question #1 answer

4._____ Question #2 answer

5._____ Task List/To Do/Question List

AUGUST TASK LIST

Check here if completed	Task	Initials
	Review of Unpaid Bills Detail Report	
	Preview customer statements	
	Review financial statements for accounts on correct statements	
	Verify cash balance on trial balance equals cash balance on bank reconciliation	
	Review trial balance for completeness and accuracy	
	Back up your monthly transactions to an external destination (e.g. flash drive), changing file name to the month	

To Do/Follow-up/Question List

September Transactions/Activities

Reminder of monthly tasks!

9/3   Planted 3 small arbor vitae and 3 boxwood bushes with 3 yards of mulch at the entrance to Nottingham Condominium complex, 16 hours. Create invoice.

9/3   Spent 8 hours on general clean-up work at Davidson Foods. Create invoice.

9/5   Placed ad in the local newspaper advertising snow plowing services, charged $27.00 on credit card.

9/7   Completed lawn maintenance for ALL contracted customers; create invoices.

9/10   Received full payment from August statements except for Brown's April invoice.

9/17   Make federal and Wisconsin estimated tax payments. (Checks #1058 and 1059.) Prepare 1040-ES and WI 1-ES.

9/21   Completed lawn maintenance for ALL contracted customers; create invoices.

9/26   Received and paid invoice #382 to American Insurance $960 and $450 for workers compensation (comp) and business insurance for October, 2013 thru March, 2014. *Edit memorized transaction. (See April transaction).*

9/27   Received fertilizer ordered from JS Supply. Terms n/30, Invoice #56.

9/30   Payroll: Mary (last month of full salary) (ck #1061)   Max: 120 hours (ck#1062)

WATCH YOUR EXCEL FILE for wage limits – Max goes over the federal unemployment wage limit this month and the employer's federal unemployment must be recalculated from September through December!

9/30   Return Mary to part-time status for remainder of year.

9/30   Perform month-end tasks.

Since it is end of quarter, print/PDF customer statements.

Credit Card Services, Inc.

D & M Yard Services

Statement Date: 9/5/2013

Amount Due: 384.00

Due Date: 9/15/2013

Charge Summary:

8/7	Gas To Go	120.00
8/17	Cell World	60.00
8/18	Gas To Go	54.00
8/26	Utility Service Corp.	150.00

XYZ Bank

D & M Yard Services

Acct. # 745-1332

9/1/2013 thru 9/30/2013

Beg. Balance: 21373.26

Deposits & CM

9/10   3928.32

Checks & DM

1052	435.20	1057	384.00
1053	965.39	1058	500.00
1054	1059.56	1059	150.00
1055	1000.00		
1056	750.00		

9/30   SC   15.00

Ending Balance: 20042.43

September Questions

1. Prepare Excel or Word report of wages for workers compensation audit: 1/1/13 through 9/30/2013. List wages, regular and overtime, <u>by employee</u> for period. Then list wages <u>by types</u>: office and landscaping/field labor. Make sure total per employee list equals total per type. Wages are reported by type because the workers comp rates are different for office versus field labor; list the workers comp code per the WI Workers Comp Code Manual.

2. As completed in March and June, see task list for quarterly comparison of control account balances to subsidiary ledger balances. Document in your Word document.

3. As a measure of internal control over sequentially numbered invoices, prepare <u>report</u> of numerically sorted invoices for quarter from the Customer Center/Transactions/Invoice.

4. Complete: a) Monthly Task List and b) your To Do/Follow-up Question List with at least two items to be addressed by your "manager"/teacher.

5. Prepare a short 3 minute oral presentation addressing 2 managerial/business-related (e.g. internal controls, marketing...) and 3 financial-related items. Submit a presentation outline. Note: instructor will select students each quarter.

CHAPTER PRINT/SUBMISSION SUMMARY

1._____ Customer statements

2._____ Check Register for July - September with Dave's initials to indicate reviewed

3._____ Subsidiary ledger reports for A/R, A/P and Inventory used in question #2

4._____ Report of numerically sorted invoices for quarter

5._____ Bank Account Reconciliation

6._____ Trial Balance

7._____ Questions #1 & 2

8._____ Outline notes for presentation

9._____ Task List/To Do/Question List

SEPTEMBER TASK LIST

Check here if completed	Task	Initials
	Review of Unpaid Bills Detail Report	
	Compare A/R control account balance (A/R on trial balance) to a detail report of the A/R subsidiary ledger	
	Compare A/P control account balance (A/P on trial balance) to a detail report of the A/P subsidiary ledger	
	Compare Inventory control account balance (Inventory on trial balance) to a detail report of the Inventory subsidiary ledger	
	Prepare report of numerically sorted invoices from the Customer Center/Transactions/Invoice	
	Review check detail for July - September, Dave indicates review with his initials on report (see cash-related information at beginning of project) Export report into Excel to note initials.	
	Review year-to-date general ledger	
	Verify cash balance on trial balance equals cash balance on bank reconciliation	
	Review trial balance	
	Back up your monthly transactions to an external destination (e.g. flash drive), changing file name to the month	

To Do/Follow-up/Question List

October Transactions/Activities

Reminder of monthly tasks!

10/3   Purchased used heavy-duty dump truck with plow for snow plowing from PP Equipment for $20,000, $500 down payment, 5%, 5-year note for remaining balance. Calculate monthly payment using PMT function in Excel and prepare amortization schedule. Monthly payments start **Nov**. 3, 2013. Use write check function to record; review journal entry (Reports/Transaction Journal).   Dump truck is not suited for personal use.

10/5   Completed lawn maintenance for ALL contracted customers and performed leaf service (additional time incurred is noted below) for all contracted customers:

Brown/Calhoun/Laxson/Garrett: 2 hours each

Forest Hill School: 4 hours

Jacksonville Industrial Park: 6 hours

Nottingham Condominium Complex: 6 hours

In addition, incurred 3 hours at Davidson Foods for fall clean-up.

Create invoices; account for leaf service in Landscaping Services and enter description of work for additional time.

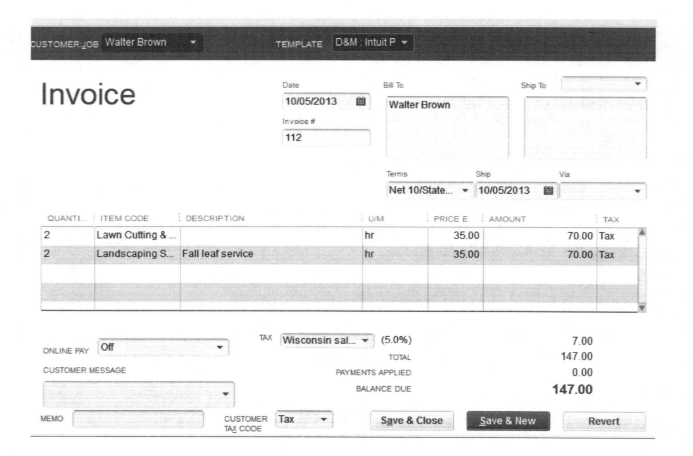

10/5 Received invoices #278 and #1289 from Healthcare Insurance and Investors, Inc. respectively, for third quarter health insurance of $1740 and 401k contributions of $321, terms: n/10 on both. We are recording the invoices here; cancel message regarding paying payroll liabilities.

10/10 Received full payment from September statements except for Brown's April invoice.

10/12 Paid $27 to Girl Scouts, $12 for cookies and $15 cash donation, with check #1066 to Ann Smith; charge to drawing account, will determine income tax impact in October questions.

10/15 Pay outstanding invoices except for PP Equipment. Reminder: quarterly WT-6 payment due. *Prepare WT-6 (Hint: refer to July transactions/activities for help).*

10/19 Completed lawn **AND** leaf maintenance (see time incurred on October 5th) for ALL and <u>ONLY</u> contracted customers (not Davidson Foods); create invoices.

10/31 Prepare monthly payroll:

Mary: 32 hours (ck #1072)   Max: 150 hours (ck #1073)

10/31 Perform month-end tasks including preparing sales tax report (ST-12) and payment of third quarter sales tax and 3rd quarter payroll reports and payments. Refer to July quarterly work if necessary. Draw will be check #1077.

Credit Card Services, Inc.

D & M Yard Services

Statement Date: 10/5/2013

Amount Due: 576.24

Due Date: 10/15/2013

Charge Summary:

9/5	Newspapers, Inc.	27.00
9/7	Gas To Go	85.00
9/10	ABC Food Store	117.24
9/17	Cell World	60.00
9/18	Gas To Go	95.00
9/20	XYZ Drug Store	42.00
9/26	Utility Service Corp.	150.00

XYZ Bank

D & M Yard Services

Acct. # 745-1332

10/1/2013 thru 10/31/2013

Beg. Balance: 20042.43

Deposits & CM

10/10   3372.70

Checks & DM

1060	1410.00	1066	27.00
1061	965.39	1067	576.24
1062	807.65	1068	1740.00
1063	1000.00	1069	321.00
1064	750.00	1070	120.00
1065	500.00	1071	157.29

10/31 SC   15.00

Ending Balance: $ 15025.56

October Questions

1. Print amortization schedule for dump truck with snow plow as carry forward document on different color paper (if possible).

2. Find the IRS publication that pertains to charitable contributions. Based on the guidelines, is the amount or part of the amount to the Girl Scouts tax deductible? Why or why not?

3. Reconcile Sales Tax Revenue Summary to sales accounts in the general ledger for 3rd quarter. Calculate total sales for *quarter* less tax exempt sales (to Forest Hill School) to equal taxable sales. Show reconciliation on sales tax liability report.

4. Compare amounts on the 3nd quarter Payroll Summary report to amounts on Excel worksheets used to complete 941 and UCT-101 and general ledger accounts. Show comparison on Payroll Summary Report exported into Excel.

5. Complete: a) Monthly Task List and b) your To Do/Follow-up Question List with at least two items to be addressed by your "manager"/teacher.

CHAPTER PRINT SUMMARY

1._____ Bank Account Reconciliation

2._____ Trial Balance

3._____ Question #1 – amortization schedule

4._____ Question #2 – charitable contribution guidelines

5._____ Sales Tax Reconciliation & ST-12 (Question #3)

6._____ Payroll Reports: WT-6, 941, UCT-101, Payroll Summary Report and comparion and Excel file (Question #4)

7._____ Task List/To Do/Question List

OCTOBER TASK LIST

Check here if completed	Task	Initials
	Review of Unpaid Bills Detail Report	
	Preview customer statements	
	Verify cash balance on trial balance equals cash balance on bank reconciliation	
	Review trial balance for completeness and accuracy	
	Back up your monthly transactions to an external destination (e.g. flash drive), changing file name to the month	

To Do/Follow-up/Question List

November Transactions/Activities

Reminder of monthly tasks!

11/1   ALL lawn maintenance customers and Davidson Foods have contracted for snow plowing and will be billed on a $45 per hour basis. In addition, D & M has contracted with new snow plowing customers, Thrifty Outlet Mall and County Hospital, from the newspaper ad.

11/3   First payment on note due today for truck with snow plow; refer to your amortization schedule for proper split between principal and interest. Check #1079.

11/5   Leaf service **ONLY**; final maintenance of year for contracted customers.

       Brown, Calhoun and Laxson: 3 hours each

Garrett:	4 hours
Davidson Foods:	6 hours
Forest Hill School:	6 hours
Jacksonville Ind. Park:	8 hours
Nottingham Condo:	8 hours

11/6   Purchased printer paper, ink and miscellaneous office supplies, charged $86.10 to credit card.

11/10 Received full payment of October balances from Davidson Foods, Forest Hill School, Jacksonville Industrial Park and Nottingham Condominium Complex.

11/22   David attended a 3-day landscaping convention in Las Vegas. Sue (wife), Mason and Jamie (son and daughter) went along to enjoy sightseeing and shopping. Total costs: airfare: $1200 (total for 4 people), hotel: $600 (a larger room for family was <u>not</u> required), and food: $270 (total for 4 people). Entire trip charged to credit card. Journalize all costs to drawing at this time.

11/28   Unexpected early snowstorm:

Brown/Calhoun/Laxson/Garrett: 1 hour each

Davidson Foods/Forest Hill School/Jacksonville Ind. Park: 2 hours each

Nottingham Condominium Complex: 4 hours

Thrifty Outlet Mall/County Hospital: 6 hours each

Create invoices! Watch sales tax treatment!

11/30   Receipts in full from: Brown (except April invoice), Calhoun, Laxson, and Garrett from October statements. Since these are the first late payments, enter a reminder comment about payment terms in the footer on the D & M Yard Services statement template for November statements. Use Intuit Standard Statement for commercial customer November statements. Print/PDF statements.

11/30   Perform month-end tasks.

Mary: 32 hours   Max: 80 hours

Reminder: watch federal unemployment!

In addition make payment to PP Equipment for another $1000 plus interest since last payment on August 15, 2013. (107 days).

Dave will take a $2000 draw this month.

Checks #1081-1084

Credit Card Services, Inc.

D & M Yard Services

Statement Date: 11/5/2013

Amount Due: $332.00

Due Date: 11/15/2013

Charge Summary:

Date	Description	Amount
10/9	Gas To Go	82.00
10/17	Cell World	60.00
10/26	Utility Service Corp.	150.00
10/27	Gas to Go	40.00

XYZ Bank

D & M Yard Services

Acct. # 745-1332

11/1/2013 thru 11/30/2013

Beg. Balance: 15025.56

Deposits & CM

11/10   2745.70

Checks & DM

1072	136.28	1076	360.82
1073	1059.56	1077	1000.00
1074	495.12	1078	750.00
1075	1574.48	1079	367.99
		1080	332.00

11/30 SC   15.00

Ending Balance: $ 11680.01

November Questions

1. Research and print the support for income tax treatment of convention costs as it pertains to the landscaping convention attended by Dave and his family. After your research, review/correct your accounting for the convention costs. Non-deductible costs should be accounted for in the drawing account and deductible costs in Miscellaneous Expense and Meals and Entertainment Expense accounts.

2. Review financial statements, Profit & Loss Standard and Balance Sheet Standard for correct classification of accounts added in the last months.

3. Complete: a) Monthly Task List and b) your To Do/Follow-up Question List with at least two items to be addressed by your "manager"/teacher.

CHAPTER PRINT/SUBMISSION SUMMARY

1._____ Customer Statements

2._____ Bank Account Reconciliation

3._____ Trial Balance

4._____ Question #1 – tax treatment of convention costs

5._____ Task List/To Do/Question List

NOVEMBER TASK LIST

Check here if completed	Task	Initials
	Review of Unpaid Bills Detail Report	
	Prepare customer statements with payment terms message	
	Review financial statements	
	Verify cash balance on trial balance equals cash balance on bank reconciliation	
	Review trial balance for completeness and accuracy	
	Back up your monthly transactions to an external destination (e.g. flash drive), changing file name to the month	

To Do/Follow-up/Question List

December Transactions/Activities

Reminder of monthly tasks!

12/6   Received full payment from November statements except for the following: Brown's April invoice, Jacksonville Industrial Park, and Larry Laxson.

12/11 Heavy snowstorm plowing:

Brown/Calhoun/Laxson:	3 hours each
Garrett:	4 hours each
Davidson Foods/Forest Hill School:	6 hours each
Jacksonville Industrial Park/Nottingham Condo:	8 hours each
Thrifty Outlet Mall/County Hospital:	8 hours each

Create invoices.

12/13 New customer, County Hospital, complained about poor snow plowing job; issued credit memo for 3 hours. Apply credit to invoice.

12/17 Purchased and received a pallet (40 50# bags) of salt from JS Garden Supply. Invoice #919, $160, terms n/30. Salt will be used for sidewalks and entry ways and billed at $6/bag.

12/24 Purchased a ham and turkey for both Mary and Max from ABC Food Store as holiday gifts, charged the business credit card, $35.32.

12/31 Perform month-end tasks. Checks: #1088-1091

Payroll: Mary: 24 hours   Max: 60 hours

These hours are through December 23, the remaining time for the year will be accounted for in a year-end accrual in the year-end tasks.

Pay remaining balance to PP Equipment with interest. (31 days)

Monthly draw to Dave, $1000.

Credit Card Services, Inc.

D & M Yard Services

Statement Date: 12/5/2013

Amount Due: 2458.10

Due Date: 12/15/2013

Charge Summary:

Date	Description	Amount
11/6	Office City	86.10
11/7	Gas To Go	42.00
11/15	Best Air	1200.00
11/17	Cell World	60.00
11/22	Win Here Inn	600.00
11/22	Convention Food Serv.	270.00
11/24	ABC Food Store	50.00
11/26	Utility Service Corp.	150.00

XYZ Bank

D & M Yard Services

Acct. # 745-1332   12/1/2013 thru 12/31/2013

Beg. Balance: $11680.01

Deposits & CM

12/1	1323.00
12/6	2094.51

Checks & DM

1081	136.28
1082	471.76
1083	1072.23
1084	2000.00
1085	750.00
1086	367.99
1087	2458.10
12/31 SC	15.00

Ending Balance: $ 7826.16

December Questions

1. Dave will make his last Federal and Wisconsin estimated income tax payments on the January 15th due date. What impact does this have on this year's income tax return? Research and print the IRS support. (Specifically, how will the WI payment impact his federal itemized deductions?)

2. Dave learns that Max has been doing snow plowing jobs on the side with company equipment. Address financial and legal impacts of this situation. What controls would help detect this activity?

3. Dave also learns that Max has been plowing Mary's driveway. Address the financial impact to D & M Yard Services as well as the impact on Mary's wages, noting the amount is deemed to be de minimus here.

4. Dave provided holiday gifts to his employees; research and print the IRS guidelines of fringe benefits to employees.

5. Complete: a) Monthly Task List and b) your To Do/Follow-up Question List with at least two items to be addressed by your "manager"/teacher.

6. Prepare a short 3 minute oral presentation addressing 2 managerial/business-related (e.g. internal controls, marketing...) and 3 financial-related items. Submit a presentation outline. Note: instructor will select students each quarter.

CHAPTER PRINT/SUBMISSION SUMMARY

1._____ Customer Balance Detail with credit memo approval (export to Excel to note initials)

2._____ Check Register for October – December, reviewed & initialed by Dave

3._____ Bank Account Reconciliation

4._____ Trial Balance

5._____ Question #1 – income tax estimates

6._____ Question #2 – side jobs

7._____ Question #3 – plowing Mary's driveway

8._____ Question #4 – employee gifts

9._____ Task List/To Do/Question List

10.____ Outline for presentation for selected students

DECEMBER TASK LIST

Check here if completed	Task	Initials
	Review of Unpaid Bills Detail Report	
	Credit memo prepared and approved	
	Review check register for October – December and submit with Dave's initials	
	Verify cash balance on trial balance equals cash balance on bank reconciliation	
	Review balance for completeness and accuracy	
	Back up your monthly transactions to an external destination (e.g. flash drive), changing file name to the month	

To Do/Follow-up/Question List

Year End Activities & Income Tax Return Preparation

<u>Note:</u> Use QuickBooks help where needed! *Add new accounts if needed.*

1. Balance Sheet Account Analysis, Adjusting Entries and Business Tax Forms: Print/PDF year-to-date general ledger to complete this analysis. *Use supplemental information provided on following pages.* Provide full explanations of adjustments and comments in one Word document, saving any forms or reports as a PDF.

   ➢ **Cash:** Verify cash balance in the general ledger agrees with reconciled balance on the December bank reconciliation
      - Comment on cash position throughout the year; make 2 suggestions to improve cash position for 2014
   ➢ **Petty Cash:** Replenish fund
   ➢ **Accounts Receivable:** Review A/R Aging Detail report, tie total of customer balances to A/R control account in general ledger. Review for past due invoices; noting the invoice date and our terms <u>from the statement date</u> (QuickBooks does not calculate the due dates correctly).
      - Prepare friendly collection letters for Jacksonville Industrial Park and Larry Laxson who did not pay in December from their November statements.

   Under Company\Prepare Letters with Envelopes:

Find Letter Templates   ✕

   QuickBooks cannot find the preinstalled letter templates in your company file folder, but letter templates do exist in your QuickBooks program folder.

   To copy the letter templates from your QuickBooks program folder, click Copy.

   If the letter templates your company uses are in a different folder on your computer, or on another computer on your network (for QuickBooks Pro users in a multi-user office), click Browse to locate the letters. The

Copy	Browse...	Cancel	Help

   Prepare Collection Letters\Active-Customers-1 day or more\Select Jacksonville and Laxson\Friendly Collection\Dave Michaels-Owner\"OK" for *QuickBooks information is missing.* Edit letter to be a reminder of payment due.

      - Write-off Brown's long outstanding uncollected account using the direct write-off method. Review QuickBooks help for write-off. Note bad debt expense should only reflect sale portion of entry. A general journal entry is necessary to adjust for the sales tax payable portion. This write-off will be accounted for on your 4th quarter Sales Tax Return. Also using Word, prepare your own short customer letter notifying Brown of this adjustment.

- On Company Snapshot create bar graph for Top Customer By Sales, submit PDF or screen shot in Word Document.

- Comment on receivable collection throughout the year; make suggestion relating to receivable management for 2014

- **Inventory:** Compare inventory balance in the general ledger (book balance) to the physical count listing; make any necessary adjustment(s) to the item's cost of goods sold account
  - Comment on inventory levels, be specific to inventory items
- **Supplies:** Review supplies inventory, make any necessary adjusting entry
- **Prepaid Insurance:** Reconcile unexpired insurance balance: in Word document calculate number of months of insurance for 2014 and compare to prepaid insurance balance; make any necessary adjusting entry
- **Security Deposit:** Determine balance is correct; comment in Word document.
- **Equipment/Trucks/Computer/Leasehold Improvements:** Calculate and record straight-line depreciation using IRS suggested lives (Use IRS Publication 946 as your guide), half-year convention with zero salvage values. We will not create a fixed asset item list.
  - Prepare subsidiary ledgers using provided asset record forms found on next pages
- **Equipment/Trucks/Computer/Leasehold Improvements** *Part 2*: In Wisconsin, businesses are also subject to a personal property tax. Research to define "personal property" that is taxable. Find the WI Statement of Personal Property return (any year); copy and paste or take a screen shot of Schedule A of the return; include in your Word document.
- **Accounts Payable:** Review A/P Aging Detail report, tie total of vendor balances to A/P control account in general ledger.
  - Research the requirements to determine which of our vendors would receive a 1099. (Hint: there are two of them!) Copy and paste this information in your Word document. Using QuickBooks help and 1099 Wizard, prepare the necessary 1099s with the amounts in the appropriate boxes and the 1096, summary page.
- **Credit Card Payable:** Reconcile balance to December statement owed in January, 2014; document in Word file.
- **Sales Tax Payable:** Prepare 4th quarter, ST-12, sales tax return; reconcile balance in Sales Tax Payable account to balance due on report (Reminder to account for write-off on Sales Returns, Allowances and Bad Debt line)
- **Notes Payable:** Compare balance in account to amortization schedule.
  - Record general journal entry to properly classify note between current and long-term liability.
  - Accrue for December interest using your amortization schedule – use interest amount for Jan. 3, 2014 payment and account for 28 days in December.

- ➢ **ALL Payroll Related Accounts:** First make sure all of Mary's wages are accounted for in Office Wage Expense.
  - ○ Accrue for payroll for last week of year: Mary 8 hours, Max 12 hours.

  - ○ Complete all 4th quarter AND year-end payroll reports, see specific reports below. Print 4th quarter Payroll Summary Report. Note no payment of payroll liabilities is made at this time; these amounts are due in January, 2014.

  - ○ 4th quarter 941: Total the 941 taxes on your Payroll Summary report, compare to 941 Summary - Excel worksheet in QuickBooks (Employees/Payroll Tax Forms/Tax Form Worksheets in Excel, *Note: if you get QB Tax Forms Password Message, cancel until message is removed*) and to balance of FICA Payable on trial balance. Go to IRS Website for Form 941(any year) and complete first page for 4th quarter, noting difference in amounts between your payroll summary and 941 summary is your current quarter's adjustment for fraction of cents.

  - ○ 4th quarter WT-6 and 2013 WT-7: Complete WT-6 and WT-7 using forms found on the Wisconsin Department of Revenue website.

  - ○ 4th quarter UCT-101: Create Tax Form Worksheet for State SUI Wage Listing for 4th quarter, multiply by state unemployment rate and compare to SUTA Payable balance in trial balance. Complete UCT-101 using form found on Wisconsin's Workforce Development website (any year) noting our wage limit is $13,000.

  - ○ 2013 940 with Schedule A: Create Tax Form Worksheet in Excel for Annual 940 with 401k as Company Paid Retirement:

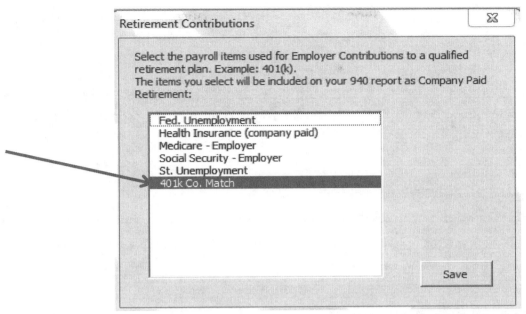

Research the purpose of Schedule A, what does this amount (credit reduction) represent, document on your Word document. Complete Form 940 and Schedule A found on the IRS website. Make the necessary adjusting entry to the FUTA Payable account.

- 2013 W-2s and W-3: Create Tax Form Worksheet for Annual W-2/W-3. Compare amounts on worksheet to Employee Earnings Summary. Show comparison of box 1 amounts for Mary, Max and Brian on Word Document. Research W-2 health insurance reporting requirements as pertains to D & M Yard Services. Note your finding on the Word Document.

- Compare balances of 401k and health insurance (employee and employer) on 4th quarter Payroll Summary Report to payable accounts on trial balance.

> **Dave Michaels, Capital:** Review for any misclassified entries
> **Dave Michaels, Drawing:** Review for any misclassified entries

2. Export financial statements into Excel, re-format Profit & Loss Standard and Balance Sheet Standard to reflect proper presentation in accordance with GAAP and professional appearance, show only year-to-date numbers, shade and bold headings. Show both QuickBooks financial statements and your edited statements on the same worksheet. Prepare 2013 Statement of Owner's Equity in Excel. Export QuickBooks Statement of Cash Flows and prepare corrected Statement of Cash Flows on same worksheet, noting QuickBooks cannot accurately account for all changes in the accounts. Submit Excel file.

3. Select 5 ratios; use only **year-end** balances when calculating ratios with "average" denominators and comment on the results. Use a variety of liquidity and profitability ratios.

4. Calculate payroll to sales ratio in two ways: first, using total of wage expense and employee benefit expense as the numerator; second, using total wage expense alone. Comment on the results.

5. QuickBooks does not have a formal year-end closing process. On the first of the new fiscal year, QuickBooks automatically closes all income and expense accounts to the default equity account, "Retained Earnings". At year-end, an entry to close the drawing account to capital would have to be journalized.

   Per the QuickBooks community help:

   QuickBooks does not have the Closing Entries in the sense that you can pull up the Journal Entries on the screen and see the credits to expenses and debits to income and credit to the Retained Earnings. When you run a report that needs to show these entries, e.g., a QuickReport on Retained Earnings, QuickBooks calculates them and displays them in the report. But you can not "QuickZoom" on them to bring them to the screen. The type will show as "Closing Entry" which is not a real transaction type in QuickBooks.

   Since we are not using the "real" current year; we will not see this process in QuickBooks, nor close the drawing account.

6. List 3 suggestions for the 2013 business plan and explain the reasoning for your suggestions. (Consider using the above ratios as a basis for your suggestions.)

7. Using Word, Excel or PowerPoint, prepare an organizational flow chart of the owner and employees with a brief list of their duties under each name on the chart; then show a second flow chart with the addition of 2 office employees and how this affects the segregation of duties, keeping in mind good internal controls. Copy and paste into yearend Word document.

8. Identify:
    a. 2 internal controls in place;
    b. 2 current weaknesses in internal control and suggest controls that should be implemented to address those weaknesses;
    c. 3 new internal controls that would need to be implemented if D & M Yard Services expanded to 10 employees, additional inventory, and an increased client base.

YEAR END PRINT/SUBMISSION SUMMARY

1._____ Word document of year end activities, e.g. comments, screen shots, ratios...

2._____ A/R:

- Jacksonville Industrial Park and Laxson collection letters
- Brown's collection letter
- Top Customer By Sales Bar Graph

3._____ Equipment/Trucks...:

- Subsidiary ledgers
- WI Statement of Personal Property Tax Return (if not screen shot)

4._____ A/P: 1099s and 1096

5._____ ST-12

6._____ Payroll-Related:

- Payroll Summary Report
- Excel files/worksheets: 941 Summary, State SUI Wage Listing, Annual 940, W-2s and W-3
- 4th quarter 941
- 4th quarter WT-6 & Annual WT-7
- 4th quarter UCT-101
- 2013 940 with Schedule A

7._____ Excel file of financial statements

8._____ Task List

YEAR END TASK LIST

Check here if completed	Task	Initials
	Verify Cash balance in the general ledger agrees with reconciled balance on the December bank reconciliation	
	Record journal entry to replenish petty cash fund	
	Compare total of A/R Aging Detail to the A/R control account balance	
	Write-off Brown's account	
	Compare Inventory balance to the physical listing; make inventory adjustment	
	Record Supplies adjusting entry	
	Reconcile Prepaid Insurance	
	Verify Security Deposit balance	
	Calculate and record depreciation	
	Complete fixed asset subsidiary ledgers	
	Compare balance to A/P control account balance	
	Prepare 4th quarter, ST-12; reconcile balance in Sales Tax Payable account to balance due on report	
	Classify Note Payable and accrue interest	
	Account for Office Wages; accrue for year-end payroll; prepare 4th quarter and year-end payroll reports; record FUTA adjusting entry: compare balances in employee benefit accounts	
	Review capital and drawing accounts for reasonableness of entries	

9. Prepare individual Federal and Wisconsin Income Tax Returns for Dave and Sue Michaels; use YOUR NAME as last name on returns using tax preparation software.

   a. If you do not have a school provided software purchase TaxACT software, "ultimate bundle" which includes federal and state editions, cost is approximately $25, select **DOWNLOAD** version
      (see http://www.taxact.com)

   b. See completed organizer and source documents on next pages

   c. Use MACRS/DDB depreciation
      i. Chevy truck GVWR is 6250# and 22,000 business miles, no personal miles. Reminder: this was not a new truck when placed into service
      ii. Note: NO Sec. 179 will be taken

   d. Reconcile the difference between D & M Yard Services net income/(net loss) per QuickBooks Profit & Loss statement and the Schedule C net profit or (loss), document on QuickBooks statement or Word document and submit with your return

   e. Understand the income tax treatment of each item; upon completion of returns, instructor will select each student to explain one item/area

   f. Save file and submit Federal and Wisconsin income tax returns

   g. Using TaxACT, calculate the federal income tax effects of taking Sec. 179 where possible *and* maximum contributions to Individual Retirement Accounts for Dave and Mary if eligible; submit Federal return ONLY

Credit Card Services, Inc.

D & M Yard Services

Statement Date: 1/5/2014

Amount Due: $617.02

Due Date: 1/15/2014

Charge Summary:

12/2	ABC Food Store	124.72	
12/4	Max's Drug Store	15.18	
12/7	Gas To Go	120.00	
12/17	Cell World	60.00	
12/18	Gas to Go	74.00	
12/24	ABC Food Store	35.32	
12/26	Utility Service Corp.	150.00	
12/27	PP Equipment	37.80	(charge to Maintenance Expense)

Physical Inventory List

Item ID	Item Description	Count	By
Arbor Vitae 36"	Arbor Vitae 36"	1	DM
Arbor Vitae 5'	Arbor Vitae 5'	0	DM
Boxwood bushes	Boxwood bushes	0	DM
Fertilizer	Fertilizer	20 bags	DM
Mulch	Bulk mulch	DNV*	DM
Seed	Grass seed	0	DM
Straw	Straw bales	0	DM
Topsoil	Screened topsoil	DNV*	DM

*DNV = did not verify
due to bulk nature of
item

Office Supply Physical Inventory List

Printer paper   2 reams at $10 each = $20

Printer ink   2 cartridges = $34

Miscellaneous $15

ASSET RECORD

DESCRIPTION:

PURCHASED FROM:

PURCHASE DATE:

COST:

DEPRECIATION METHOD:

ESTIMATED LIFE:

ASSET BALANCE   ACCUMULATED DEPRECIATION

Date	Desc.	Debit Amt.	Credit Amt.	Balance

Date		Debit Amt.	Credit Amt.	Accum. Deprec. Balance	**NET ASSET BOOK VALUE**

ASSET RECORD

DESCRIPTION:

PURCHASED FROM:

PURCHASE DATE:

COST:

DEPRECIATION METHOD:

ESTIMATED LIFE:

ASSET BALANCE   ACCUMULATED DEPRECIATION

Date	Desc.	Debit Amt.	Credit Amt.	Balance

Date		Debit Amt.	Credit Amt.	Accum. Deprec. Balance	**NET ASSET BOOK VALUE**

ASSET RECORD

DESCRIPTION:

PURCHASED FROM:

PURCHASE DATE:

COST:

DEPRECIATION METHOD:

ESTIMATED LIFE:

ASSET BALANCE

Date	Desc.	Debit Amt.	Credit Amt.	Balance

ACCUMULATED DEPRECIATION

Date		Debit Amt.	Credit Amt.	Accum. Deprec. Balance	NET ASSET BOOK VALUE

ASSET RECORD

DESCRIPTION:

PURCHASED FROM:

PURCHASE DATE:

COST:

DEPRECIATION METHOD:

ESTIMATED LIFE:

ASSET BALANCE

Date	Desc.	Debit Amt.	Credit Amt.	Balance

ACCUMULATED DEPRECIATION

Date		Debit Amt.	Credit Amt.	Accum. Deprec. Balance	NET ASSET BOOK VALUE

ASSET RECORD

DESCRIPTION:

PURCHASED FROM:

PURCHASE DATE:

COST:

DEPRECIATION METHOD:

ESTIMATED LIFE:

ASSET BALANCE				
Date	Desc.	Debit Amt.	Credit Amt.	Balance

ACCUMULATED DEPRECIATION				Accum. Deprec. Balance	**NET ASSET BOOK VALUE**
Date		Debit Amt.	Credit Amt.		

ASSET RECORD

DESCRIPTION:

PURCHASED FROM:

PURCHASE DATE:

COST:

DEPRECIATION METHOD:

ESTIMATED LIFE:

ASSET BALANCE				
Date	Desc.	Debit Amt.	Credit Amt.	Balance

ACCUMULATED DEPRECIATION				Accum. Deprec. Balance	**NET ASSET BOOK VALUE**
Date		Debit Amt.	Credit Amt.		

2013 Client Tax Organizer (Prepared by Tax Client)

★ Indicates source document attached.

1. Personal Information

	Name	Soc. Sec. No.	Date of Birth	Occupation	Work Phone
Taxpayer	David A. Michaels	388-22-6666	8/14/64	Self-employed	
Spouse	Sue G. Michaels	360-24-9781	6/26/66	Admin. Asst.	

Street Address	City	State	ZIP	County
800 Main St.	Landscape	WI	53022	Winnebago

	Taxpayer	**Spouse**	**Marital Status**		
Blind	☐Yes ☒No	☐Yes ☒No	☒Married	Will file jointly	☒Yes ☐No
Disabled	☐Yes ☒No	☐Yes ☒No	☐Single		
Pres. Campaign Fund	☐Yes ☒No	☐Yes ☒No	☐Widow(er), Date of Spouse's Death _____		

2. Dependents (Children & Others)

Name (First, Last)	Relationship	Date of Birth	Social Security Number	Months Lived With You	Disabled	Full Time Student	Dependent's Gross Income
Mason Michaels	Son	5/21/02	550-65-9944	12		X	---
Jamie Michaels	Daughter	7/8/04	251-85-6333	12		X	---
Dolly Weatherspoon(1)	Sue's mother	8/12/30	397-82-5531		Blind		22,140 total

(1) Dolly lives in an assisted living facility. Dave & Sue provided over one-half of Dolly's support. (Determine Dolly's dependency status; no other income tax effect.)

Please provide all statements (W-2s, 1098s, 1099s, etc.)

Please answer the following questions to determine maximum deductions

1. Are you self-employed or do you receive hobby income? ☒Yes ☐No

2. Did you receive income from raising animals or crops? ☐Yes ☒No

3. Did you receive rent from real estate or other property? ☒Yes ☐No

4. Did you receive income from gravel, timber, minerals, oil, gas, copyrights, patents? ☐Yes ☒No

5. Did you withdraw or write checks from a mutual fund? ☐Yes ☒No

6. Do you have a foreign bank account, trust, or business? ☐Yes ☒No

7. Do you provide a home for or help support anyone not listed in Section 2 above? ☐Yes ☒No

8. Did you receive any correspondence from the IRS or State Department of Taxation? ☐Yes ☒No

9. Were there any births, deaths, marriages, divorces or adoptions to your related family? ☒Yes ☐No

10. Did you give a gift of more than $13,000 to one or more people? ☐Yes ☒No

11. Did you have any debts cancelled, forgiven, or refinanced? ☐Yes ☒No

12. Did you go through bankruptcy proceedings? ☐Yes ☒No

13. If you paid rent, how much did you pay? Was heat included? ☐Yes ☒No

14. Did you pay interest on a student loan for yourself, your spouse, or your dependent during the year? ☐Yes ☒No

15. Did you pay expenses for yourself, your spouse, or your dependent to attend classes beyond high school? ☒Yes ☐No

16. Did you have any children under the age of 19 or 19 to 23 year old students with unearned income of more than $950? ☐Yes ☒No

17. Did you purchase a new alternative technology vehicle or electric vehicle? ☐Yes ☒No

18. Did you install any energy property to your residence such as solar water heaters, generators or fuel cells or energy efficient improvements such as exterior doors or windows, insulation, heat pumps, furnaces, central air conditioners or water heaters? ☐Yes ☒No

19. Did you own $50,000 or more in foreign financial assets? ☐Yes ☒No

3. Wage, Salary Income

Attach W-2s:

Employer	Taxpayer	Spouse
★General Manufacturing	☐	☒
	☐	☐
	☐	☐
	☐	☐

4. Interest Income

Attach 1099-INT, Form 1097-BTC & broker statements

Payer	Amount
★Educators Credit Union	754.08
★Winnebago Bank	30.89
Tax Exempt	
U.S. Savings Bond (cash not received)	$200

5. Dividend Income

From Mutual Funds & Stocks – Attach 1099-DIV

Payer	Ordinary	Capital Gains	Non-Taxable
★American Funds	169.98	40.00	1.00

6. Partnership, Trust, Estate Income

List payers of partnership, limited partnership, S-corporation, trust, or estate income – Attach K-1

7. Property Sold

Attach 1099-S and closing statements

Property	Date Acquired	Cost & Imp.	Sold
Personal Residence			
Vacation Home			
Land →★WI Dells (See attorney stmt.)	1/2/2005	5,000	4/6/13
Other –Personal car, sold for $1,000	3/2/2008	7,600	10/5/13

8. I.R.A. (Individual Retirement Acct.)

Contributions for tax year income

	Amount	Date	√ for Roth
Taxpayer			
Spouse			

Amounts withdrawn. Attach 1099-R & 5498

Plan Trustee	Reason for Withdrawal	Reinvested?
		☐Yes ☐No
		☐Yes ☐No
		☐Yes ☐No
		☐Yes ☐No

9. Pension, Annuity Income

Attach 1099-R Payer*	Reason for Withdrawal	Reinvested?
		☐Yes ☐No
		☐Yes ☐No
		☐Yes ☐No
		☐Yes ☐No

* Provide statements from employer or insurance company with information on cost of or contributions to plan.

Did you receive	Taxpayer	Spouse
Social Security Benefits	☐Yes ☒No	☐Yes ☒No
Railroad Retirement	☐Yes ☒No	☐Yes ☒No

Attach SSA 1099, RRB 1099

10. Investments Sold

Stocks, Bonds, Mutual Funds, Gold Silver, Partnership Interest—Attach 1099-B & confirmation slips

Investment	Date Acquired/Sold		Cost	Sale Price
★Widget, Inc.	1/8/95 /	9/5/2013	1,090.00	1,100.00
★Standard Products	2/8/98 /	5/8/2013	5,526.00	3,822.00

11. Other Income

List all Other Income (including non-taxable)	
Alimony	
Child Support	
Scholarship (Grants) (Sue)	500
★Unemployment Compensation (Sue)	1825
Prizes, Bonuses, Awards	
★Gambling, Lottery (expenses _170_)	2000
Unreported Tips	
Director / Executor's Fee	
Commissions	
Jury Duty	
Worker's Compensation	
Disability Income	
Veteran's Pension	
Payments from Prior Installment Sale	
★State Income Tax Refund	1275
Other : Inheritance (Sue's uncle)	10000

12. Medical/Dental Expenses

Medical Insurance Premiums (paid by you)	
Prescription Drugs	310
Insulin	
Glasses, Contacts	475
Hearing Aids, Batteries	
Braces	
Medical Equipment, Supplies	
Nursing Care	
Medical Therapy	
Hospital	
Doctor/Dental/Orthodontist	
Mileage (no. of miles)	
Miles after June 30	

13. Taxes

Real Property Tax 1)★Residence	4045.46
2) Cabin in Northern WI	600.00
Other: –Telephone excise tax	100
– 2012 Federal Income Tax	500
–WI sales tax not pd on out-of-state purchases	19

14. Interest Expense

★Mortgage interest paid (attach 1098)	5000.59
Interest paid to individual for your home (include amortization schedule)	
Paid to:	
Name _____	
Address _____	
Social Security No. _____	
Investment interest	
Premiums paid or accrued for qualified mortgage insurance	
Other: MasterCard	150

15. Casualty/Theft Loss

For property damaged by storm, water, fire, accident, or stolen.

Location of Property _____

Description of Property _____

	Other	Federally Declared Disaster Losses
Amount of Damage		
Insurance Reimbursement		
Repair Costs		
Federal Grants Received		

16. Charitable Contributions

	Other	
★Church	705	
United Way	25	
Scouts	12	Cookies bought by D & M Yard Services
University, Public TV/Radio		
Heart, Lung, Cancer, etc.	30	(Includes $15 to Girl Scouts by D & M Yard Services)
Wildlife Fund		
★Salvation Army, Goodwill	350	See donation receipt.
Other: Political Party	300	
Non-Cash _____		
Volunteer (no. of miles) _____ @.14		

17. Child & Other Dependent Care Expenses

Name of Care Provider	Address	Soc. Sec. No. or Employer ID	Amount Paid

Also complete this section if you receive dependent care benefits from your employer.

18. Job-Related Moving Expenses

Date of move _____

Move Household Goods	_____
Lodging During Move	_____
Travel to New Home (no. of miles)	_____
Miles after June 30	_____

19. Employment Related Expenses That You Paid (Not self-employed)

Dues—Union, Professional (Sue)	240
Books, Subscriptions, Supplies	_____
Licenses	_____
Tools, Equipment, Safety Equipment	_____
Uniforms (include cleaning)	_____
Sales Expense, Gifts	_____
Tuition, Books (work related) (Sue - ___	782

Began pursuing associates degree in
accounting; took 1 evening class.
Winnebago County Technical College
700 Main St., Landscape, WI 53022
39-0043212

Entertainment	_____
Office in Home:	_____
In Square feet: a) Total Home _____	_____
b) Office _____	_____
c) Storage _____	_____
Rent	_____
Insurance	_____
Utilities	_____
Maintenance	_____

20. Investment-Related Expenses

Tax Preparation Fee (300 for personal part of return; 200 for Schedule C/business; 100 for Schedule E/rental.)	600
Mutual Fund Fee	_____
Safe Deposit Box Rental	120

21. Business Mileage

Do you have written records?	☒Yes	☐No
Did you sell or trade in a car used for business?	☐Yes	☒No

If yes, attach a copy of purchase agreement

Make/Year Vehicle: (Information in D & M Yard Services)

Date purchased	_____
Total miles (personal & business)	_____
Business miles (not to and from work)	_____
Miles after June 30	_____
From first to second job	_____
Miles after June 30	_____
Education (one way, work to school)	_____
Job Seeking	_____
Other Business	_____
Round Trip commuting distance	_____
Gas, Oil, Lubrication	_____
Batteries, Tires, etc.	_____
Repairs	_____
Wash	_____
Insurance	_____
Interest	_____
Lease Payments	_____
Garage Rent	_____

22. Business Travel

If you are not reimbursed for exact amount, give total expenses.*

Airfare, Train, etc.	_____
Lodging	_____
Meals (no. of days _____)	_____
Taxi, Car Rental	_____
Other	_____
Reimbursement Received	_____

*Business Convention to Las Vegas (see D & M Yard Services' financial statements)

23. Estimated Tax Paid

Due Date	Date Paid	Federal	State
	Apr 15	500	150
	June 15	500	150
	Sept 15	500	150
	Jan 15	500	150

24. Education Expenses

Student's Name	Type of Expense	Amount
Sue Michaels	Books	182
	Tuition	600

—— Note: Books __not__ required to
—— be purchased from the school.

25. Other Deductions

Alimony / Child Support: Pd. to David's ex-wife $3,600
(ex-wife claims dependent)

Social Security No. _____ $ _____
Student Interest Paid $ _____
Health Savings Account Contributions $ _____
Archer Medical Savings Acct. Contributions $ _____

26. Questions, Comments, & Other Information

See D & M Yard Services for business
income/expense

Residence:
Town _____ County _Winnebago_____
Village _____ School District _1862____
City _Landscape_____ _____

27. Direct Deposit of Refund / or Savings Bond Purchases

Would you like to have your refund(s) directly deposited into your account?   ☒Yes   ☐No

ACCOUNT

Owner of account	☐Taxpayer	☐Spouse	☒Joint

Type of account   ☐ Checking   ☒ Traditional Savings   ☐ Traditional IRA   ☐ Roth IRA
   ☐ Archer MSA Savings   ☐ Coverdell Education Savings   ☐ HSA Savings   ☐ SEP IRA

Name of financial institution __Educators Credit Union__
Financial Institution Routing Transit Number (if known) __123456__
Your account number __120356__

Supplemental information:

RENTAL PROPERTY

Address:	123 W. South St.	
	Landscape, WI 53022	
Rents:	$12,000	Purchased property & placed into service 4/1/2003
Insurance:	159	for $80,000 total, $15,000 allocated to land
★Mtg. Interest:	6,971.93	
Repairs:	242	Purchased refrigerator 7/5/2013 $1,200
★Real Estate Tax:	4,210.80	
Utilities:	182	
		Vehicle info: 2004 Chevrolet Impala
		purchased 7/8/2007
		10,000 total miles driven in 2013
		(700 rental-related miles)

To the best of my knowledge the information enclosed in this client tax organizer is correct and includes all income, deductions, and other information necessary for the preparation of this year's income tax returns for which I have adequate records.

Dave Michaels	2/20/2014	*Sue Michaels*	2/20/2014
Taxpayer	**Date**	**Spouse**	**Date**

Self-employed	Administrative Assistant
Occupation	**Occupation**

★Indicates source document attached.

FACTS ABOUT YOUR 2013 SOCIAL SECURITY BENEFIT STATEMENT

This is your 2013 Social Security Benefit Statement. Use it, along with the information below, to see if part of your Social Security benefits may be taxable.

What You Need to Do

Determine whether any of your Social Security benefits are taxable.

Box 2—"Social Security Number"—shows the Social Security number of the person shown in Box 1.

Box 3—"Benefits Paid in 2013"—shows the total amount paid to you in 2013.

SEE IRS PUBLICATION 915 FOR FULL DESCRIPTION OF BOXES ON SSA-1099.

Box 4—"Benefits Repaid to SSA in 2013"—shows the total amount of benefits you repaid us in 2013.

FORM SSA-1099—SOCIAL SECURITY BENEFIT STATEMENT

2013	PART OF YOUR SOCIAL SECURITY BENEFITS SHOWN IN BOX 5 MAY BE TAXABLE INCOME. SEE THE REVERSE FOR MORE INFORMATION.

Box 1. Name Dolly Weatherspoon	Box 2. Beneficiary's Social Security Number 397-82-5531

Box 3. Benefits Paid in 2013 21990.30	Box 4. Benefits Repaid to SSA in 2013 NONE	Box 5. Net Benefits for 2013 (Box 3 minus Box 4) 21990.30

DESCRIPTION OF AMOUNTS IN BOX 3		Description of Amount in Box 4
Paid by check or direct deposit	$19,914.00	NONE
Medicare Part B premiums deducted from your benefits	$2,076.30	
Total Additions	$21,990.30	**Box 6. Voluntary Federal Income Tax Withheld** NONE
Benefits for 2013	$21,990.30	**Box 7. Address**

Box 8. Claim Number *(Use this number if you need to contact SSA.)*

Form SSA-1099-SM (1-2013)   DO NOT RETURN THIS FORM TO SSA OR IRS

PAYER'S name, street address, city, state, ZIP code, and telephone no.		Payer's RTN (optional)	OMB No. 1545-0112	**Interest Income**
Bank of America P.O. Box 2 Anywhere, CA 55222		**1** Interest Income $ 150	20**13**	
		2 Early withdrawal penalty $	Form **1099-INT**	
PAYER'S federal identification number 16-1234567	RECIPIENT'S identification number 397-82-5531	**3** Interest on U.S. Savings Bonds and Treas. Obligations $		Copy B For Recipient
RECIPIENT'S name Dolly Weatherspoon		**4** Federal income tax withheld $	**5** Investment expenses $	This is important tax information and is being furnished to the Internal Revenue Service. If you are required to file a return, a negligence penalty or other sanction may be imposed on you if this income is taxable and the IRS determines that it has not been reported.
Street address (including apt. no.) 800 Main St		**6** Foreign tax paid $	**7** Foreign country or U.S. possession	
City, state, and ZIP code Landscape, WI 53022		**8** Tax-exempt interest $	**9** Specified private activity bond interest $	
Account number (see instructions)		**10** Tax-exempt bond CUSIP no.	**11** State	**12** State identification no.	**13** State tax withheld $

Form **1099-INT**   (keep for your records)   Department of the Treasury – Internal Revenue Service

175

22222	Void ☐	**a** Employee's social security number 360-24-9781	For Official use Only ➤ OMB No. 1545-0008		

b Employer identification number (EIN) 14-0689340	**1** Wages, tips, other compensation 76,707.24	**2** Federal income tax withheld 8,623.39
c Employer's name, address, and ZIP code	**3** Social security wages 83,869.53	**4** social security tax withheld 3,522.52
General Manufacturing P.O. Box 60300 Ft. Myers, FL 33906	**5** Medicare wages and tips 83,869.53	**6** Medicare tax withheld 1,216.11
	7 Social security tips	**8** Allocated tips
d Control number	**9**	**10** Dependent care benefits

e Employee's first name and initial	Last name	Suff.	**11** Nonqualified plans	**12a** See instructions for box 12
Sue G	Michaels			

13 Statutory employee ☐ Retirement plan ☒ Third-party sick pay ☐

14 Other	**12b** DD	12,910.16

f Employee's address and ZIP code
800 Main St
Landscape, WI 53022

12c C 171.93

12d D 7,162.29

15 State	Employer's state ID number	**16** State wages, tips, etc.	**17** State income tax	**18** Local wages, tips, etc.	**19** Local income tax	**20** Locality Name
WI	761015	76,707.24	4,709.91			

Form **W-2**	Wage and Tax Statement	2013	Department of the Treasury—Internal Revenue Service For Privacy Act and Paperwork Reduction Act Notice, see the separate instructions.
Copy C For Employee's Records.			Cat. No. 10134D

Do Not Cut, Fold, or Staple Forms on This Page

☐ CORRECTED (if checked)

PAYER'S name, street address, city, state, ZIP code, and telephone no.	Payer's RTN (optional)	OMB No. 1545-0112	
EDUCATORS CREDIT UNION **1400 N NEWMAN RD** **RACINE WI 53406** **262-886-5900**	**1** Interest Income $ 754.08	$20\mathbf{13}$	**Interest Income**
	2 Early withdrawal penalty $ .00	Form **1099-INT**	

PAYER'S federal identification number **39-0555293**	RECIPIENT'S identification number 388-22-6666	**3** Interest on U.S. Savings Bonds and Treas. Obligations $ .00	**Copy B** **For Recipient**
RECIPIENT'S name, street address (including apt. no.), city, state, and ZIP code David and Sue Michaels 800 Main Street Landscape, WI 53022		**4** Federal income tax withheld $ .00	**5** Investment expenses $ .00	This is important tax information and is being furnished to the Internal Revenue Service. If you are required to file a return, a negligence penalty or other sanction may be imposed on you if this income is taxable and the IRS determines that it has not been reported.
		6 Foreign tax paid $ .00	**7** Foreign country or U.S. possession	
		8 Tax-exempt interest $ .00	**9** Specified private activity bond interest $ .00	
Account number (see instructions) 120356		**10** Tax-exempt bond CUSIP no. (see instructions)	

Form **1099-INT**   (keep for your records)   Department of the Treasury – Internal Revenue Service

	Payer's identifying number	**1** Interest income not included in Box 3
WINNEBAGO BANK P.O. BOX 648 LANDSCAPE, WI 53022	39-0734270	30.89
	Recipient's identifying number	**2** Early withdrawal penalty
	39-1212121	.00
	PAYER'S RTN (OPTIONAL)	**3** Interest on U.S. Savings Bonds and Treas. obligations
CORRECTED (if checked) ☐	0759-01341	.00

If your taxpayer identifying number is not shown or is incorrectly shown, please furnish the correct number to the payer.

TO WHOM PAID ➤

OMB No. 1545-0112

2013

Interest Income
Copy B
For Recipient
FORM 1099 INTEREST
SUBSTITUTE

D & M Yard Services
900 Main Street
Landscape, WI 53022

This is important tax information and is being furnished to the Internal Revenue Service. If you are required to file a return, a negligence penalty or other sanction may be imposed on you if this income is taxable and the IRS determines that it has not been reported.

4 Federal income tax withheld
.00

5 Foreign tax paid
.00

6 Foreign country or U.S. possession
.00

Keep this copy for your records

INTEREST STATEMENT FOR

TYPE	ACCOUNT NUMBER	INTEREST EARNED	FORFEITURE	FEDERAL TAX WITHHELD
STMT SUPER SAVER ACCOUNT		30.89	.00	.00

American Funds®

PO Box 6007
Indianapolis IN 46206-6007

Recipient's name and address

> David and Sue Michaels
> 800 Main Street
> Landscape, WI 53022

Form 1099-DIV

OMB No 1545-0110

2013 Dividends | **Copy B**
and Distributions | For Recipient

Payer's name, address and telephone number
American Funds Service Company
PO Box 6007
Indianapolis IN 46206-6007
800-421-4225

Recipient's identification number:

388-22-6666

- This is important tax information and is being furnished to the Internal Revenue Service (IRS). Please keep for your records.
- If you are required to file a return, a negligence penalty or other sanction may be imposed on you if this income is taxable and the IRS determines that it has not been reported.

Payer's (Fund's) name and federal identification number	Recipient's account and fund number	1a	Total ordinary dividends	1b	Qualified dividends	2a	Total capital gain distributions	4	Federal income tax withheld	6	Foreign tax paid
THE INVESTMENT COMPANY OF AMERICA 95-1426645			169.98		169.98		40.00		0.00		N/A

See Next Page for State Tax Exclusion

American Funds®

State tax exclusions for U.S. government income worksheet

Worksheet results

Fund name	Ordinary dividend	x	U.S. government factor	=	Your U.S. government income
The Investment Company of America®	$169.98		0.0043		$0.73

Your total state tax exclusion: $0.73

To determine your individual tax situation, please consult your tax adviser.

Legal Services of America

4/6/2013

TO: Dave and Sue Michaels
                800 Main St.
                Landscape, WI 53022

Services rendered for Wisconsin Dells land sale closing $500

(Land sale gross proceeds of $8,000)

☐ VOID   ☐ CORRECTED

FILER'S name, street address, city or town, province or state, country, ZIP or foreign postal code, and telephone number. **Legal Services of America** **123 Main Street** **Landscape, WI, US 53022**	**1** Date of Closing 4/6/2013	OMB No. 1545-0997 20**13** Form **1099-S**	**Proceeds From Real Estate Transactions**
	2 Gross Proceeds $ 8,000		

FILER'S federal identification number 39-7532681	TRANSFEROR'S Identification Number 388-22-6666	**3** Address or legal description (including city, state and ZIP code)	**Copy B** **For Recipient**
TRANSFEROR'S name **Dave & Sue Michaels**		**Lot 82** **Wisconsin Dells, WI 53965**	This is important tax information and is being furnished to the Internal Revenue Service. If you are required to file a return, a negligence penalty or other sanction may be imposed on you if this income is taxable and the IRS determines that it has not been reported.
Street address (including apt. no.) **800 Main Street**			
City or town, province or state, country, and ZIP or foreign postal code **Landscape, WI, US, 53022**		**4** Check here if the transferor received or will receive property or services part of the consideration ▶ ☐	
Account or escrow number (see instructions)		**5** Buyer's part of real estate tax $ --	

Form **1099-S**

NOTE: 1099-S is correct form for reporting, however will use 1099-B in Tax Act.

1 Gross winnings	2 Federal Income tax withheld
2,000.00	**0.00**
3 Type of wager	4 Date won
$ 0.05	**11 06 2013**
5 Transaction	6 Slots
1000275818	**Slots**
7 Winnings from identical wagers	8 Cashier
	S. Roaf

PAYER's name, address and zip code

Potawatomi Bingo Casino
1721 W. Canal St.
Milwaukee, WI 53223

Federal identification number	Telephone number
39-1693007	**8007297244**
9 Winner's taxpayer ID number	10 Window
	8
11 First ID	12 Second ID
360-24-9781	
13 State/Payer's state ID number	14 State income tax withheld
WI 036102042076003	**0.00**
WINNER'S name and address:	15 City income tax withheld

Sue Michaels
800 Main St
Landscape, WI 53022

Under penalties of perjury, I declare that, to the best of my knowledge and belief, the name, address, and taxpayer identification number that I have furnished correctly identify me as the recipient of this payment and any payments from identical wagers, and that no other person is entitled to any part of these payments

Signature   **Date**

➤   *Sue Michaels*   ➤ **11/06/2013**

Form W-2G Certain Gambling Winnings	**2013**

For Privacy and Paperwork Reduction Act Notice and instructions for completing this form, see the 2013 General Instructions for Certain Information Returns.

PAYER'S name, address, ZIP code	
Wisconsin Department of Revenue Mail Stop 5-77 PO Box 7878 Madison, WI 53708-7878 Payer's Federal Identification Number: **39-6006491** **RECIPIENT'S name** David and Sue Michaels 800 Main Street Landscape, WI 53022	Form 1099-G **2013** **Certain Government Payments** Refund is for tax year: **2013** Recipient's Tax Account Recipient's Identification Number: Number: 001-1023698246-02 388-22-6666 **Computation of State Tax Refund:** Refund Requested 1,275.00 • **State Income Tax** **Refund:** **$1,275.00**

This is important tax information and is being furnished to the Internal Revenue Service. **If you are required to file a return, a negligence penalty or other sanction may be imposed on you if this income is taxable and the IRS determines that it has not been reported.** Federal law requires all states to provide a Form 1099-G if you receive, or received the benefit of, a state income tax refund.

What is this form?
- This is information about your Wisconsin income tax refund for 2012.
- It is not a refund. This refund was already issued to you in 2013.
- It is not a bill. You do not owe the amount shown.
- If you use a tax preparer, give this form to him/her with all of your other tax documents. A tax preparer will know how to use this information when filing your federal income tax return.

Why did I receive this form?
- Your Wisconsin Income tax refund may be taxable income on your federal tax return, if you itemized deductions on Schedule A of a prior year federal tax return.
- Usually the refund in box 1 is the same as the refund that was issued to you. It may be different if:
  - All or part of your refund was used for next year's estimated tax,
  - You reported sales and use tax or donated all or part of your refund,
  - You received certain credits that are not refunds of income tax,
  - You were charged penalties, interest, or a late filing fee, or
  - All or part of your refund was used to pay a debt you owed.

What should I do with this form if I prepare my own tax returns?
- Use the instructions for federal Form 1040, line 10 to compute the taxable refund amount
- This refund amount is not taxable on your Wisconsin tax return
  - If you file Form 1, subtract this amount from your federal income on line 6
  - If you file Form 1A, do not include this amount as income

Go paperless
- This form is now available online from our confidential website. It's free, simple and secure!
- Sign up at revenue.wi.gov – click 'Form 1099-G'. We will email you when the forms are posted

Wisconsin Department of Revenue	Internal Revenue Service
• www.revenue.wi.gov – search 1099G • Dor1099G@revenue.wi.gov • (608) 266-2486	• www.irs.gove • 1-800-829-1040 toll-free

(NOTE: This amount is fully taxable.)

TOWN OF   LANDSCAPE   Tear at Perforation; Return Top Portion With Payment   2013 REAL PROPERTY TAX BILL

Assessed Value Land 115,000	Assessed Value Improvements 185,000	Total Assessed Value 300,000	Ave. Assmt. Ratio 1.0063	Net Assessed Value Rate (Does NOT reflect Lottery Credit) 13.9704/M
Est. Fair Mkt. Land 114,300	Est. Fair Mkt. Improvements 183,800	Est. Fair Mkt. 298,100	A star in this box means unpaid prior year taxes.	School taxes reduced by school levy tax credit 433.18

Taxing Jurisdiction	Last Year Est. State Aids Allocated Tax District	This Year Est. State Aids Allocated Tax District	Last Year Net Tax	This Year Net Tax	% Tax Change
STATE OF WISCONSIN			50.53	50.59	.1
COUNTY OF WINNEBAGO	110,417	100,169	669.93	674.41	2.2
TOWN OF LANDSCAPE	319,200	269,609	776.27	777.93	.2
SCHOOL DISTRICT 1862	6,569,787	5,978,140	2,295.85	2,315.13	.8
WINNEBAGO TECH COLLEGE	106,176	79,552	367.31	373.06	1.6
Total	7,105,580	6,427.470	4,149.89	4,191.12	1.0
		First Dollar Credit	63.23	62.69	.9-
		Lottery and Gaming Credit	79.73	82.97	4.1
TAX KEY		Net Property Tax	4,006.93	4,045.46	1.0

Make Check Payable to: TOWN OF LANDSCAPE KATHY KARALEWITZ, TREASURER W320S8315 Beulah Rd Landscape, WI 53022	Full payment Due On or Before January 31, 2014 **$4,045.46**
	First Installment Due On or Before January 31, 2014 **$1,981.46**
When paying after January 31, 2014 Make Check Payable to: WINNEBAGO COUNTY TREASURER 515 W MORELAND BLVD, ROOM 148 LANDSCAPE WI 53022	Second Installment Due On or Before July 31, 2014 **$2,064.00**
	TOTAL DUE FOR FULL PAYMENT PAY BY January 31, 2014 **$4,045.46** Warning: If not paid by due date, installment option is lost and total tax is delinquent and subject to interest and penalty (See Reverse).
Property Address: 800 Main Street Landscape, WI 53022	

O
T
H
E
R

PAID
12/29/2013
$4,045.46

| RECIPIENT'S/LENDER'S name, address and telephone number 01/10/14 | *Caution: The amount shown may not be fully deductible by you. Limits based on the loan amount and the cost and value of the secured property may apply. Also, you may only deduct interest to the extent it was incurred by you, actually paid by you, and not reimbursed by another person. | OMB No. 1545-0901 **2013** Substitute Form 1098 | MORTGAGE INTEREST STATEMENT |

Wells Fargo Bank, N.A.
Return Mail Operations
PO Box 14411
Des Moines, IA 50306-3411

We accept telecommunications relay service calls.
Fax #: 1-866-278-1179   ☐ CORRECTED (if checked)
Phone #: 1-866-234-8271
PAYER'S/BORROWER'S name, street address, city, state, and ZIP code

David and Sue Michaels
800 Main Street
Landscape, WI 53022

Copy B
For *Payer*

The information in boxes 1, 2, 3, and 4 is important tax information and is being furnished to the internal Revenue Service. If you are required to file a return, a negligence penalty or other sanction may be imposed on you if the IRS determines that an underpayment of tax results because you overstated a deduction for this mortgage interest or for these points or because you did not report this refund of interest on your return.

RECIPIENT Federal identification no.
94-1347393

PAYER'S SOCIAL SECURITY number
388-22-6666

1. Mortgage interest received from Payer(s)/borrower(s)	$5,000.59
2. Points paid on purchase of principle residence (See Box 2 on back)	$0.00
3. Refund of overpaid interest (See Box 3 on back.)	$0.00
4. Mortgage Insurance Premiums	$0.00
Account number (optional)	5 Real Estate Taxes $0.00

Form 1098 Substitute   SEE BACK SIDE FOR IMPORTANT INFORMATION (Keep for your records.)   Department of the Treasury – Internal Revenue Service

Please consult a Tax Advisor about the deductibility of any payments made by you or others.

Principal reconciliation	Property Address
$87,082.35 Beginning balance $17,651.07 Principal applied $69,431.28 Ending balance	800 Main Street Landscape, WI 53022
	$1,198.86 Total current payment

---2013 INTEREST DETAIL---

TOTAL INTEREST APPLIED 2013 $5,000.59
2013 MORTGAGE INTEREST RECEIVED FROM PAYER/BORROWER(S) $5,000.59

If you have questions about your loan, you can use our automated "Personal Mortgage Information Line" at the toll free number listed at the top of this statement. By selecting one of the options listed, you can receive information regarding:

  – Taxes paid year-to-date
  – The amount & date of your last payment
  – Interest paid year-to-date
  – Other valuable information

Wells Fargo Home Mortgage, a division of Wells Fargo Bank, N.A., believes Customers come first. You can always count on us to provide the excellent service you've come to expect.

NCW

Goodwill

Serving North Central Wisconsin Communities

Donor Name ___Sue Michaels___

Address: ___800 Main St, Landscape, WI 53022___

Date: ___06/19/13___ Attendant: ___J. Gilson___

Your donations support our programs and services in your community

- ❏ Antigo
- ❏ Ashwaubenon
- ❏ Darboy
- ❏ Eau Claire
- ❏ Grand Chute
- ❏ Green Bay East

- ❏ Green Bay West
- ❏ La Crosse
- ❏ Manitowoc
- ❏ Marshfield
- ❏ Menasha
- ❏ Menomonie

- ❏ Onalaska
- ❏ Oshkosh
- ❏ Rhinelander
- ❏ Rice Lake
- ❏ Shawano
- ❏ Stevens Pt

- ❏ Tomah
- ❏ Waupaca
- ❏ Weston
- ❏ Wis Rapids
- ❏ E-Commerce

Thank you for increasing your Goodwill

Because Goodwill NCW is a not-for-profit, 501(c)(3) human services organization, your donation is tax deductible. Use this form as your donation receipt. *See back for guidelines.*

$ _____ Clothing - men's		$ _____ Jewelry
$ _350_ Clothing - women's		$ _____ Books, toys, games
$ _____ Clothing - children's		$ _____ Sporting goods
$ _____ Shoes/boots/sandals		$ _____ Tools
$ _____ Housewares		$ _____ Small appliances
$ _____ Dishes and glassware		$ _____ Small furniture items
$ _____ Other _____		

Value (as determined by donor*) $ _____

*For more donation information ask for our *Donating to Goodwill* brochure, or see our Web site: www.goodwillncw.org

Note: This is confirmation that you did not receive any goods or services in exchange for this donation.

Goodwill NCW, 1800 Appleton Road, Menasha, WI 54952

Divine Redeemer Lutheran Church
31385 W. Hill Road
Hartland, WI 53029

David and Sue Michaels
800 Main Street
Landscape, WI 53022

Contributions for the period of 1/1/2013 through 12/31/2013
Total: $705.00

This is your 2013 Contribution Statement. No goods or services were provided to the donor other than intangible religious benefits. Please contact the business office at 262-367-8400 if you have any questions.

General Fund (1)   Fund Total: **$705.00**

Pledge: (none)

Date	Amount	Description	Date	Amount	Description
1/09/13	40.00		1/23/13	40.00	
2/06/13	25.00		2/20/13	40.00	
2/27/13	20.00		3/13/13	25.00	
3/27/13	40.00		4/10/13	30.00	
4/17/13	20.00		4/24/13	25.00	
5/01/13	25.00		6/05/13	40.00	
6/26/13	25.00		7/10/13	40.00	
7/17/13	20.00		7/31/13	30.00	
8/21/13	20.00		9/18/13	40.00	
9/25/13	20.00		10/02/13	20.00	
10/23/13	20.00		10/30/13	20.00	
11/27/13	20.00		11/27/13	20.00	
12/11/13	20.00		12/18/13	20.00	

☐ VOID ☐ CORRECTED

RECIPIENT'S/LENDER'S name, address, and telephone number		OMB No. 1545-0901	Mortgage Interest Statement
Norwest Mortgage P. O. Box 2222 Chicago, IL 87211		20**13** Form **1098**	

RECIPIENT'S federal identification no. 95-2318940	PAYER'S social security number 388-22-6666	**1** Mortgage Interest received from payer(s)/borrower(s) $ 6,971.93	**Copy B** **For**
PAYER'S/BORROWER'S name David and Sue Michaels		**2** Points paid on purchase of principal residence $	**Payer** For Privacy Act and Paperwork
Street address (including apt. no.) 800 Main Street		**3** Refund of overpaid interest $	Reduction Act Notice, see the **2013 General**
City, state, and ZIP code Landscape, WI 53022		**4** Property Address: 123 W. South St. Landscape, WI 53022	**Instructions for** **Certain** **Information**
Account number (see instructions)			**Returns**

Form **1098**   Department of the Treasury – Internal Revenue Service

201

PAY 1ST INSTALLMENT OR IN FULL TO:

TOWN TREASURER
BORIS SABATKE

STATE OF WISCONSIN
PROPERTY TAX BILL FOR
REAL ESTATE

Correspondence should refer to tax number.
See reverse side for important information.

Assessed Value Land	Assessed Value Improvements	Total Assessed Value	Ave. Assmt. Ratio	Est. Fair Mkt. Land	Est. Fair Mkt. Improvements	Total Est. Fair Mkt.
25,000	130,000	155,100	78.32%	31,900	166,100	198,000

☐ A star in the box means unpaid prior year taxes.

	Net Property Tax	3,835.80
	DELQ UTILITI	375.00

Taxing Jurisdiction #3	Last Year Est. State Aids Allocated Tax Dist.	This Year Est. State Aids Allocated Tax Dist.	Last Year Net Tax	This Year Net Tax	% Tax Change
STATE OF WISCONSIN	223,330	218,039	36.98	39.67	7.3
WINNEBAGO COUNTY	258,580	246,225	799.40	850.55	6.4
TOWN OF LANDSCAPE	412,467	394,392	647.47	646.36	.2–
WINNEBAGO SCHOOL	27,773	26,484	1,894.44	2,091.66	10.4
TECH DIST			252.32	265.03	5.0
Total	922,150	885,140	3,630.61	3,893.27	7.2
	Lottery Credit		83.48	57.47	31.2–
	Net Property Tax		3,547.13	3,835.80	8.1

Net Assessed Value Rate
(Does NOT reflect lottery credit)
025101663

School taxes reduced by
school levy tax credit   386.28

TOTAL DUE   FOR FULL PAYMENT

PAY BY JANUARY 31 NEXT YEAR TO LOCAL TREASURER

$ 4,210.80

Warning: If not paid by due dates, installment option is lost and total tax is delinquent subject to interest and if applicable, penalty. (See reverse.)

Or Pay 1st Installment
TO LOCAL TREASURER
$ 2,264.80
BY: January 31, 2014

And Pay 2nd Installment
TO COUNTY TREASURER
$ 1,946.00
BY: July 31, 2014

IMPORTANT: Be sure this description covers your property. This description is for property tax bill only and may not be a full legal description.

Property Address:
123 W. South St.
Landscape, WI 53022

Special Charge Paid	
Special Assessment Paid	
Property Tax Paid	
Paid by	Rec'd by

Special Tax Paid	
Total Amount Paid	
Balance Due	
	Date

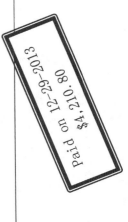

Paid on 12-29-2013
$4,210.80

203

HOUSE COMPANY, INC.

100 Franklin Street, Cranston, R.I.

MEMBERS NEW YORK STOCK EXCHANGE, AMERICAN STOCK EXCHANGE

YOU BOUGHT	YOU SOLD	DESCRIPTION	1	8	1995	$ 1,090	00
75		Widget Inc., Common, $13.75		TRADE DATE		NET AMOUNT	
		New York Stock Exchange					

$ 1,031	25	$	58	75	David Michaels	706102
AMOUNT		COMMISSION			800 Main Street	YOUR ACCOUNT NUMBER
					Landscape, WI 53022	

DELIVERYING OF SECURITIES SOLD AND PAYMENT FOR SECURITIES PURCHASED MUST BE MADE BY SETTLEMENT DATE TO AVOID CHARGES FOR PREMIUMS

HOUSE COMPANY, INC.

100 Franklin Street, Cranston, R.I.

MEMBERS NEW YORK STOCK EXCHANGE, AMERICAN STOCK EXCHANGE

YOU BOUGHT	YOU SOLD	DESCRIPTION	9	5	2013	$ 1,100	00
	75	Widget Inc., Common, $15.50		TRADE DATE		NET AMOUNT	
		New York Stock Exchange					

$ 1,162	50	$	62	50	David Michaels	706102
AMOUNT		COMMISSION			800 Main Street	YOUR ACCOUNT NUMBER
					Landscape, WI 53022	

DELIVERYING OF SECURITIES SOLD AND PAYMENT FOR SECURITIES PURCHASED MUST BE MADE BY SETTLEMENT DATE TO AVOID CHARGES FOR PREMIUMS

HOUSE COMPANY, INC.

100 Franklin Street, Cranston, R.I.

MEMBERS NEW YORK STOCK EXCHANGE, AMERICAN STOCK EXCHANGE

YOU BOUGHT	YOU SOLD	DESCRIPTION	2	8	1998	$ 5,526	00
300		Standard Products, Common, $18.00 American Stock Exchange		TRADE DATE		NET AMOUNT	

$ 5,400	00	$	126	00	David Michaels	706102
AMOUNT		COMMISSION			800 Main Street	YOUR ACCOUNT NUMBER
					Landscape, WI 53022	

DELIVERYING OF SECURITIES SOLD AND PAYMENT FOR SECURITIES PURCHASED MUST BE MADE BY SETTLEMENT DATE TO AVOID CHARGES FOR PREMIUMS

HOUSE COMPANY, INC.

100 Franklin Street, Cranston, R.I.

MEMBERS NEW YORK STOCK EXCHANGE, AMERICAN STOCK EXCHANGE

YOU BOUGHT	YOU SOLD	DESCRIPTION	5	8	2013	$ 3,822	00
	300	Standard Products, Common, $13.00 American Stock Exchange		TRADE DATE		NET AMOUNT	

$ 3,900	00	$	78	00	David Michaels	706102
AMOUNT		COMMISSION			800 Main Street	YOUR ACCOUNT NUMBER
					Landscape, WI 53022	

DELIVERYING OF SECURITIES SOLD AND PAYMENT FOR SECURITIES PURCHASED MUST BE MADE BY SETTLEMENT DATE TO AVOID CHARGES FOR PREMIUMS

PAYER'S name, street address, city, state, ZIP code, and telephone no.	**1** Unemployment Compensation	OMB No. 1545-0120	**Certain Government Payments**
Wisconsin Dept. of Labor P.O. Box 89 Madison, WI 51160	**$** 1825	20**13**	
	2 State or local income tax refunds, credits, or offsets $	Form **1099-G**	

PAYER'S federal identification number	RECIPIENT'S identification number	**3** Box 2 amount is for tax year $	**4** Federal income tax withheld $	**Copy 1**
39-7654321	360-24-9781			

RECIPIENT'S name	**5** RTAA payments	**6** Taxable grants	
Susan Michaels	$	$	
Street address (including apt. no.) 800 Main St	**7** Agriculture payments $	**8** Check if box 2 is trade or business income ▶ ☐	
	9 Market gain		
City, state, and ZIP code Landscape, WI 53022	$		

Account number (see instructions)	**10a** State WI	**10b** State identification no.	**11** State income tax withheld

Form **1099-G**